Black Mirror

The Complete Episode Guide

Nick Naughton

Contents

5 - Introduction
6 - Series 1
6 - The National Anthem
12 - Fifteen Million Merits
17 - The Entire History of You
22 - Series 2
22 - Be Right Back
26 - White Bear
31 - The Waldo Moment
35 - 2014 Special - White Christmas
40 - Series 3
40 - Nosedive
44 - Playtest
48 - Shut Up and Dance
52 - San Junipero
56 - Men Against Fire
60 - Hated in the Nation
64 - Series 4
64 - USS Callister
69 - Arkangel
72 - Crocodile
76 - Hang the DJ
80 - Metalhead
84 - Black Museum
88 - Interactive Film - Bandersnatch
93 - Series 5
93 - Striking Vipers
98 - Smithereens
101 - Rachel, Jack and Ashley, Too
105 - Series 6
105 - Joan Is Awful
109 - Loch Henry
114 - Beyond the Sea
118 - Mazey Day

121 - Demon 79
125 - Series 7
125 - Common People
129 - Bête Noire
133 - Hotel Reverie
137 - Plaything
141 - Eulogy
145 - USS Callister: Into Infinity

150 - Photo Credit

INTRODUCTION

Black Mirror began way back   in
with an episode called The N   ne
minister having sexual relat   a
kidnapped member of the royal family. Although the early
episodes are very highly regarded (some feel the show was
never quite the same when it moved to Netflix) few who
watched The National Anthem would have predicted that Black
Mirror would still be going in 2025 and successfully establish a
fairly wide international audience. Fantasy anthology shows are
nothing new and seemed to be especially popular in the 60s,
70s and 80s. Twilight Zone, Outer Limits, Alfred Hitchcock
Presents, Night Gallery, One Step Beyond, Thriller, Journey to
the Unknown, Ghost Story, Beasts, A Ghost Story for
Christmas, Tales from the Darkside, Tales from the Crypt,
Monsters, Perversions of Science, Tales of the Unexpected,
Hammer House of Horror, Hammer House of Mystery &
Suspense, Ray Bradbury Theater, Amazing Stories etc, etc. The
list goes on and on.

There are a number of factors to explain why Black Mirror
managed to establish itself in such a familiar and venerable
genre. A key factor was Black Mirror shrewdly finding its own
niche and identity within this genre. Black Mirror is - in the
broadest sense - a dark anthology show about technology. Not
every episode of Black Mirror is about technology and not
every episode of Black Mirror is bleak and dystopian but bleak
stories about near future technology (sometimes plausible and
sometimes fantastical) are what put the show on the map and
what we generally expect when we tune in to watch. The remit
of Black Mirror, as far as it has a remit, has been stretched and
experimented with over time but the technology theme is still a
big part of Black Mirror's identity. Another salient factor in
Black Mirror's success is that while anthology shows are still
around it hasn't exactly been a vintage time for them of late.

Black Mirror is not being compared to Alfred Hitchcock or the original Twilight Zone or Outer Limits. The other (fantasy/horror) anthology shows during the Black Mirror years have been things like Creepshow, a forgettable Twilight Zone revival, and Channel Zero.

The greatest anthology show of modern times away from Black Mirror is Inside No.9, but that brilliant BBC show is very British and never got much fame or attention outside of its home country. Black Mirror, thanks to the Netflix platform, was able to get a wider audience and it also broadened its appeal with American based stories and famous guest stars.

Black Mirror has therefore enjoyed certain advantages but it would not have lasted so long if it wasn't good. Episodes like White Bear, White Christmas, San Junipero and USS Callister are justifiably lauded as modern anthology television classics. As we'll shall see though not every episode of Black Mirror was a home run and there are plenty of episodes too which seem to divide opinion. That's one of the interesting things about Black Mirror. There is no clear consensus when it comes to rankings. Subjective lists of the best episodes can fluctuate wildly. In the book that follows we will go through every episode of Black Mirror and examine what worked and what didn't. We'll look at the themes, subtexts and influences too. It goes without saying that what follows is merely my own opinion and may differ from your own personal ranking of the episodes. That's fine though because it's all part of the fun of anthology shows.

SERIES 1 (2011)

THE NATIONAL ANTHEM

(Directed by Otto Bathurst, Written by Charlie Brooker)

SYNOPSIS - A popular royal named Princess Susannah (Lydia Wilson) is kidnapped. The kidnapper (who obviously keeps his identity hidden) demands that Princess Susannah will only be released if the prime minister Michael Callow (Rory Kinnear) has sex with a pig on live television. If this becomes the only way to save Princess Susannah will the prime minister actually go through with it?

REVIEW - The National Anthem was the first ever episode of Black Mirror. Choosing this as the first episode was an interesting decision to say the least because you suspect it might have driven a fair few viewers away! Though the episode is quite well regarded The National Anthem - with its bestiality theme - is definitely not going to be everyone's cup of tea. Despite the ludicrous nature of this premise, The National Anthem is played straight and the ramifications of this highly distasteful and strange scenario and ransom demand are explored. The prime minister - naturally - explores every option to avoid the bestial ransom demand but the kidnapper turns out to be a lot shrewder and elusive than expected. There is also the not inconsiderable question of public opinion. How far is this prime minister really willing to go to secure Susannah's release and his own poll ratings? Well, in this story he is forced to go all the way.

The National Anthem was apparently an idea Charlie Brooker had stewing for a long time. His original idea had the beloved late celebrity Sir Terry Wogan forced to have sex with an animal but this eventually changed into a more political sort of story. The early work of Charlie Brooker often went in more for shock value - hence the grim 'high concept' of this story. It is doubtful he'd write a Black Mirror story like this today.

A big inspiration for The National Anthem was the case of Gordon Brown and Gillian Duffy. In 2010, Gordon Brown was the prime minister and campaigning (badly) for the impending general election. On the stump in Rochdale, he ended up chatting to a pensioner named Gillian Duffy. Duffy had been a Labour supporter her whole life. In her brief chat with the prime minister she complained about levels of immigration and the state of the economy. When he got in his car and drove off with his aides, the bungling Brown had forgotten to remove his mic so his private conversation was picked up by radio feeds. In his car he berated his aides for making him meet Duffy and basically called her a stupid bigoted woman. It was certainly a revealing insight into what politicians really think of the great unwashed - even the ones who actually vote for them. Brown was castigated for this incident and for the sake of the polls had to go and personally apologise to Gillian Duffy in grovelling fashion. The Brown/Duffy affair was certainly a vague inspiration for The National Anthem then in that ambitious politicians are at the mercy of public opinion - sometimes to the extent that they are forced to do things they really don't want to do. Paying a humiliating visit to Gillian Duffy to apologise in front of TV cameras was probably the last thing Brown wanted to do but he had no choice because an election was coming up and he would have been toast if he hadn't (not that Brown won the election anyway).

Another big theme in The National Anthem is the morbid fascination with what you might describe as underground material. The base and tasteless. The horrible. If the BBC put live executions on once a week I'm pretty sure those live executions would probably beat Blankety Blank and Doctor Who in the ratings. Imagine a hypothetical scenario where the prime minister has to have sex with an animal on live television. Though you'd like to think otherwise the ratings would probably be through the roof. But a lot of the people who watched would probably feel ashamed of themselves afterwards. The National Anthem is well aware of this duality. The National Anthem is quite an atypical sort of Black Mirror episode but the theme of technology being a curse as much as it might be a blessing is very prevalent. The prime minister and his team are seeking to quash this ransom demand story and resolve the matter as soon as possible but technology makes that impossible. How do you censor and hide things in the internet age? With great difficulty is the answer. One is reminded of the recent example of the New Yorker article about the Lucy Letby (the nurse convicted of murdering babies in a Cheshire hospital) case being blocked in Britain because she still faced retrials for some of her charges. Anyone in Britain who was interested in the case though could easily read the offending article online if they looked hard enough and circumnavigate the ban. Trying to suppress information in the modern world is complex and difficult.

The National Anthem is sort of like an episode of 24 or Spooks crossed with The Thick of It and then sloshed with a liberal sprinkling of Chris Morris style anything goes absurdity and black comedy. The story is surprisingly plausible for a good chunk of the running time (despite the fact that in reality the government has an official policy of not negotiating with terrorists and no prime minister in their right mind would have actually gone through with the ransom demand - no matter what the fallout might be from such a refusal) although the ultimate denouement doesn't feel very credible. In reality it is rather hard to believe that a politician would have intercourse with an animal on live television and then resume their political career as if nothing had happened! If one was the participant/victim in such a scenario - whatever the circumstances or motivation or indeed result of your actions - you'd probably never show your face in public again.

I suppose the most basic message in The National Anthem is that politicians will sometimes do anything to further their career. This is not strictly true though. Politicians, however much we may dislike a great many of them, do have their limits. If such a ransom scenario happened in real life Sir Kier Starmer is not going to have relations with a pig on television. The National Anthem is basically then a grim sort of fantasy episode with some cynical jabs at politics and a commentary on the herd like qualities of public opinion.

The National Anthem is not my favourite episode of this show and not something I tend to rush back to watch again (the bestiality theme is icky and unpleasant and betrays the more juvenile 'shock' quality to Brooker's early work) but it is a solid and gripping drama for what it is and has a fine supporting cast with the likes of Lindsay Duncan and Donald Sumpter. When people say they prefer the early Channel 4 very British version of Black Mirror it is episodes like The National Anthem they are probably thinking about. That dark and depressing sort of quality which felt very Black Mirror. It wasn't really until the Netflix years that Black Mirror gave us some more optimistic and sentimental sort of stories and even some happy endings.

What is interesting about the viewing figures for season one of Black Mirror in Britain is that The National Anthem accrued over two million viewers and then the following week's episode (Fifteen Million Merits) slumped to 1.5 million - losing over half a million viewers from the previous week. You probably don't need to be Columbo to work out why there was a drop. A lot of people watched The National Anthem and went - thanks but no thanks, this show is gross. The National Anthem is unpleasant in places and won't be for everyone but the bleak absurdity of the premise is also the reason why many like this episode a lot. The next episode would be very different - which is hardly surprising because, lest we forget, this is an anthology show!

There was a method to the madness when it comes to The National Anthem because Charlie Brooker said they deliberately chose to have a wild and controversial sort of concept in the first episode as a sort of means to give the show some publicity and get people talking. Although the viewing figures dipped after this initial story you could argue that The National Anthem did its job because this did become an infamous episode of the show and one that people definitely wouldn't forget in a hurry. So you could say that The National Anthem laid for the foundations for Black Mirror. Though not exactly a blueprint for the type of episode you would get in the future (The National Anthem is something of a one-off) it did indicate that all bets would occasionally be off in Black Mirror and this was a show that could take you to some surprising places. In a television landscape where shows can sometimes be samey and safe this was an interesting and effective hook for the show going forward. It made people feel that with Black Mirror they stood a chance of getting something very different and perhaps even unique from time to time.

The ransom demand in The National Anthem turns out to be the work of an artist named Carlton Bloom. Bloom releases Princess Susannah before the prime minister has sex with the pig but news of this doesn't travel fast enough to stop Callow going through with the act. Over a billion people watch the live broadcast and Bloom commits suicide. His worst fears about humanity have been confirmed. His grotesque 'performance art' was treated by the public as something akin to a live football match. Everyone was complicit. The public soon forget about the broadcast and go back to their lives. The prime minister has a poll boost. But by the end of the episode his marriage is broken beyond repair. He is the person who paid the biggest price.

One of the interesting things about this episode is that we have to put ourselves in the position of the prime minister. If we were in his position we definitely wouldn't go through with the ransom demand. No way. But what if a life was on the line? Would we go through with the act with the pig to save a life? Well, a lot of us still probably wouldn't go through with the act - not even to save Princess Susannah. It is not saving a life that primarily motivates the prime minister though. It is his public reputation and his family. So this story has a deeper cynical subtext about politicians.

One potential plot hole in this episode is that Bloom sends the authorities a finger as proof he has Princess Susannah. It turns out to be one of his own fingers he cut off. One would presume the authorities would be able - through DNA testing - to establish this was not really Princess Susannah's finger. The National Anthem, as it edges ever closer to its grim and shocking conclusion, becomes quite uncomfortable to watch - which is though the point. We, the viewer, are also becoming complicit in this dreadful performance art stunt. The National Anthem is what you might describe as morbidly compelling. It is horrible but we can't turn away - a lot like the people watching the act the prime minister is forced to take part in. This episode is weird and quite unpleasant in the end but it is well made and well acted. Though not to all tastes it set a dark 'all bets are off' sort of template for Black Mirror that the show sometimes struggled to live up to and sometimes patently wasn't interested in living up to anyway. Though the show would run for several more seasons there was nothing quite like The National Anthem ever again. And this is why it was chosen as the first episode. To get people talking and give Black Mirror plenty of publicity. The National Anthem, for better or worse, is a memorable entrance for Black Mirror and put the show firmly on the map.

FIFTEEN MILLION MERITS

(Directed by Euros Lyn, Written by Charlie Brooker & Kanak Huq)

SYNOPSIS - Fifteen Million Merits depicts a nightmarish future world where a group of people in a Big Brother style compound are constantly surrounded by entertainment screens pumping out porn, prank shows and reality television. They live in some sort of constrictive underground high-tech facility and must peddle bikes to generate electricity and thus earn money for essentials and also extra entertainment options on the screens which cover the walls of the tiny rooms they sleep in. They appear to be virtual prisoners in this tedious little world and the only means of escape is to be get hired on one of the moronic talent shows being pumped into their rooms 24/7. "Bing" Madsen (Daniel Kaluuya) decides that he will use the 'merits' he has earned on the exercise bikes to help Abi Khan (Jessica Brown Findlay) enter a talent show called Hot Shot. Bing has taken a shine to Abi and also noticed that she has a lovely singing voice. However, things do not quite go the way Bing might have hoped...

REVIEW - Fifteen Million Merits is the first Black Mirror episode which feels like the broad stereotype of a Black Mirror episode. The technology and digital landscape depicted here is sort of like our world except MORE - much more. This is also the first overtly dystopian story in the show. The world in Fifteen Million Merits is apparently some sort of near future society where people are confined to bunkers or silos. We never get this world explained or see outside. It could be the case that some nuclear or ecological disaster has occurred but we simply don't know. Maybe there is still a world outside but these people are not permitted to go there? It's up to the viewer to fill in the blanks for themselves. The characters in this world seem to be pretty low on the class system - but some of them do look down their nose at the cleaners so have the illusion of being mildly important or privileged even if they are not. These poor blighters having to peddle on bikes all day for little reward is an obvious commentary on the often pointless drudgery of work. How many of us, at some point in our lives, have done some tedious low-wage job that did little to alter our financial circumstances?

So most of us can, in a roundabout sort of way, relate to the characters in Fifteen Million Merits trapped in this little hamster wheel existence that seems to go nowhere. It is never even made clear in this story if all the furious bike peddling is actually accomplishing anything or merely a ruse to keep these people occupied. So you could describe this episode as Kafkaesque in the way it sets up this little nightmare world where nothing seems to make much sense. This episode was co-written by Charlie Brooker's wife Konnie Huq (billed as Kanak Huq on the credits). Konnie Huq is best known in Britain as a former presenter on the famous kids TV show Blue Peter, but she later had a stint as a presenter on The Xtra Factor - which was a companion show to The X Factor. The X Factor, as you hardly need reminded, is a singing talent show presided over by Simon Cowell. Talent shows of this ilk are hardly a new idea. Decades ago there were shows like Opportunity Knocks and The Gong Show. The X factor (and others) dusted off this ancient format and gave it a modern twist. This format was now slicker but also nastier - with more sarcasm and ruthlessness expected of the judging. Some people find these shows distasteful in the way they reduce contestants to the status of performing monkeys to be mocked and judged but there are never any shortage of participants willing to try their hand and take that shot (however unlikely) at instant fame.

Fifteen Million Merits riffs on the modern talent show landscape of television with Rupert Everett's Judge Hope on Hot Shot clearly inspired by Cowell. Konnie Huq said her experience of X-Factor opened her eyes to the fact there seem to be vast swathes of young people who have no other ambition but to be famous - even if they don't appear to have any obvious talent to facilitate this goal. Who needs qualifications or a trade if you intend to be famous? The real world holds no appeal for these fame hungry day dreamers. And this is where reality television and talent shows come in. They offer a small fleeting window of opportunity which doesn't exist in the real world. A means of potential escape from harsh reality. Thanks to Bing saving up his merits, Abi is able to get a ticket to sing on the talent show Hot Spot. Her performance of Anyone Who Knows What Love Is (Will Understand) - which will become a recurring theme song of Black Mirror and features in White

Christmas, Men Against Fire, Crocodile, Rachel, Jack and Ashley Too, Joan is Awful and Common People - goes down well but this all counts for nothing in the end. The judges imply they simply don't have room for another good singer because they already have plenty of those. Being a good singer is not an especially prized commodity in this society it seems. They don't appear to have room or an appetite for too many of them.

Judge Wraith (Ashley Thomas) suggests instead that, as an alternative to being a singer, Abi become a 'Wraithbabe' - one of the performers on his porn channel. Wraith is not interested in singers but he is always on the lookout for young women to turn into porn performers. The onlooking Bing is mortified by this turn of events but Abi, in a vulnerable state thanks to some sort of sedative (Cuppliance) she has been given as a drink agrees. So it transpires that Abi's only means of escape from the hamster wheel is to do porn. In a sense then, Fifteen Million Merits is even more relevant today in the age of OnlyFans - where women can make much more money taking their clothes off than they might have done singing or acting or working a regular job. Abi has become nothing more than a commodity. Nothing more than flesh on a screen. Despite her talent as a singer and nice personality she is only useful to this grim society as fresh meat on Wraithbabes. So this episode continues the bleak Black mirror aura established by The National Anthem.

Fifteen Million Merits shows that you don't need a huge budget to make a good episode of Black Mirror. This episode has quite a constrictive feel and is very studio bound but it is well designed and atmospheric and the nightmarish near future society it depicts is strangely believable. It doesn't feel as if we are too far off this society ourselves. Living standards have collapsed and culture becomes ever more moronic. Bing is distraught when Abi is dragooned into becoming a porn star. He is forced to watch commercials for Wraithbases featuring Abi in his room on the screens which surround him. If he tries to cover his ears a high pitched screech is deployed and he can't look away because the screens follow him around. This is a truly horrific detail. If we watch YouTube or television most of us mute the commercials or simply look at something else while we wait for whatever annoying advert is playing to end. What if you were forced to watch all the commercials though? What if you didn't have the option to avoid them? That would be horrific wouldn't it? Being forced to watch every single moronic commercial. The chilling thing about this detail in Fifteen Million Merits is that we know companies and advertisers in our own (real) society would love to do this if they could! There are websites where the commercials follow you down the screen if you scroll down. Fifteen Million Merits presents this advertising tactic and amplifies it to a terrifying degree.

So you could say that Fifteen Million Merits, like the best Black Mirror stories, works as a sort of five minutes into the future nightmare. This is science fiction but not science fiction which feels implausible. You just take the worst instincts of corporations and technology companies and picture what they will be like a few years down the line. Fifteen Million Merits clearly takes some inspiration from the Mike Judge film Idiocracy with its depiction of a dumbed down society which is fed the lowest common denominator when it comes to entertainment. It's a landscape which doesn't seem far-fetched at all when you peruse the television channels on a Saturday night. The characters in Fifteen Million Merits are trapped in a mindless soul-destroying world of pornography, commercials and reality television. The shallow society they are forced to endure mirrors some of the more mindless aspects of our own. Bing vainly attempts to shatter this world, or at least deliver a few home truths, by saving up to get on Hot Shot himself. Once on stage he threatens to kill himself with a shard of glass and launches an impassioned speech castigating the judges and this world for (to borrow an old phrase) knowing the price of everything and the value of nothing.

Rather than shatter this society with truth bombs, Bing is rewarded with his own show - where he dispenses these rants against the system for entertainment. He, just like Abi, has been commodified. His rants are not changing anything. The system is merely patronising him. Bing now has more lavish quarters - the virtual screen now depicting a forest rather than pornography or a moronic prank show. Bing has sold out. There is no escape. He has swapped one prison for another. Fifteen Million Merits, oddly, was initially judged to be quite a weak episode of the show by critics but has grown in stature over the years as Black Mirror has run and run. While the episode is not wholly original and takes on some rather obvious targets it does have a lot of Black Mirror essence with its downbeat aura and the absurd system technology has imposed on these people. Daniel Kaluuya and Jessica Brown Findlay are good as the two leads and there are memorable supporting turns by the likes of Julia Davis and Rupert Everett. Over time this has come to be seen as one of the strongest episodes in the show and gives you more or less all you would expect from an early Black Mirror episode. It's a nightmarish look at the worst aspects of our society through the prism of a near future that we may or may not manage to avoid ourselves.

THE ENTIRE HISTORY OF YOU

(Directed by Brian Welsh, Written by Jesse Armstrong)

SYNOPSIS - In the future people are implanted with a device called a 'grain' which records everything they see and hear. This gives them the ability to play back old memories and events and see them exactly as they occurred. So you can basically rewind back through your life and watch the recording (from your POV obviously) of any given moment you witnessed. A lawyer named Liam Foxwell (Toby Kebbell) attends a party with his wife Ffion (Jodie Whittaker) and becomes aware and irritated by the chemistry and familiarity she seems to have with the suave Jonas (Tom Cullen). Liam becomes more and more paranoid and jealous about what might have happened between Ffion and Jonas - the thought that his child might not even be his own but rather that of Jonas eventually becoming his ultimate fear. Ffion insists that Liam is being paranoid but is she telling the truth? The 'grain' technology provides the increasingly frazzled Liam with a possible way to find out...

REVIEW - This episode was written by Jesse Armstrong of Peep Show and Succession fame. There is though none of the humour in The Entire History of You we've come to expect from Armstrong's work. This is a bleak episode which revolves around a crumbling relationship and Liam's futile and doomed attempt to retrospectively gain some sort of control over every aspect of his wife's past. The moral of this story is that technology has its limits. What's done is done and no matter how clever our inventions become they can't rewrite the past. And if you forensically trawl through the past in obsessive fashion the chances are you are going to find something you don't like in the end. So this episode is basically then a relationship drama with a technological theme as opposed to an overt science fiction or horror/fantasy episode. The acting is good in this episode - especially Jodie Whittaker as Ffion. This episode came out six years before Whittaker was cast as the Thirteenth Doctor in Doctor Who. Whittaker got her fair share of criticism for what was an underwhelming era of Doctor Who but The Entire History of You indicates she is an accomplished supporting actor and probably better suited to that than being someone you'd stick front and centre as the lead of a show.

The grain technology in this story is an implant which goes behind the ear. The ramifications of this technology are mentioned early on when Liam learns that law firms are using it for cases where people are taking legal action against their parents for not showing them enough love when they were children! Liam is troubled by the ethics of this application but will go on to use the technology in a way that one might argue is equally troubling. The Entire History of You is the earliest example of what you might argue is a mild weakness in Black Mirror - and something which does occasionally become a trifle grating in the show. Black Mirror is not very good at depicting realistic ordinary people - to the extent that we rarely see them in the show. The characters in Black Mirror are more often than not upper middle class and catalogue model handsome. These people are not hugely relatable. They live in luxurious houses, have posh dinner parties, and work in professional occupations or the arts or in some swanky office. The characters in the show often represent this little metropolitan well heeled bubble of the type that Charlie Brooker is presumably very familiar with.

Rod Serling's The Twilight Zone, which was obviously a huge influence on Black Mirror, was better at doing stories which depicted (for want of a better phrase) the 'little man' - examples of which include Time Enough at Last, A Stop at Willoughby, Miniature, A Passage for Trumpet and Night of the Meek. This is not to say that Black Mirror never depicts more ordinary people (the main protagonists of episodes like, to pluck a couple of episodes at random, Shut Up and Dance and Demon 79 are working class) but all the same you wouldn't say this was Charlie Brooker's wheelhouse or comfort zone. It isn't a major drawback to the show but it is something which is worth mentioning. One could obviously counter this by saying this quality is perhaps sometimes very deliberate for that Black Mirror ambiance and residue. The architecture in the show is often detached, aloof and cold - a quality we find in some of the characters too. The Entire History of You owes something to the Francis Ford Coppola film The Conversation - where Gene Hackman's surveillance expert becomes a paranoid frazzled mess thanks to the very technology that he makes a living from. Liam will travel down a similar path in Black Mirror. The ability to freeze frame every moment of your past and to scrutinise still images looking for clues in words or expressions becomes a sensory overload for his state of mind.

Charlie Brooker said the moral of this story is that Liam should probably have stopped looking at the past because he was never going to like the answers waiting there for him. Toby Kebbell does well in this episode because Liam is not exactly a sympathetic character. One interesting detail in this story is that one needs to have a 'grain' implant to gain access to certain services. So, for example, if you contact the police they'll only accept the call if you have a grain implant to make it easier for them to access evidence in a criminal case. This works as a sort of commentary on our own ever changing world - where in the end you'll probably need a smartphone and electronic ID to do something preposterously mundane like buy a loaf of bread. The Entire History of You works all the better as a story because Liam is actually proved to be right about his wife. He isn't delusional or on a wild goose chase. This doesn't condone the things he does in this episode but it does prove that his instincts were right. The way he acted on his suspicions was wrong but the suspicions themselves were not. The relatively short 45 minute running time of this episode is an advantage because The Entire History of You - which is quite intense and depressing - may well have overstayed its welcome in a longer format. In this more compact length it works well as a relationship story with a technology theme.

The 'grains' in The Entire History of You are similar to how people log or display a great deal of pointless stuff online or through their phones. The world doesn't need to know every boring detail of your life. We don't care what you had for lunch today and we don't need a photograph of it either. The characters in this story have every millisecond of their life logged and ready to be played back. But is this healthy? While it might be highly useful in specific circumstances (a memory of a lost loved one or evidence if one were the victim of a crime for example) this technology would, if you became addicted to it, have the potential to drive you mad. Living in the past is fine for a few wistful moments but it isn't a place you can stay in for very long. The Entire History of You also obviously touches on the ethics of recording literally everything you see around you.

So when people use the 'grain' to replay things there are going to be people in the footage who haven't given permission to be used - not that they have any say in the matter anyway given that this technology seems to be all but mandatory. The Entire History of You is not exactly a barrel of laughs (this IS Black Mirror!) and not an easy watch but it is a strong and thoughtful drama with some interesting ruminations on the nature of memory and the ethics of technology.

One interesting thing about The Entire History of You is how it hints at a possible happy ending. Liam decides to remove his grain implant at the end. People in this society without grain implants are second class citizens but it could be the case that they are the sensible ones and will be happier. You could perhaps draw an analogy between removing the grain and people in our society who do not own a mobile telephone or don't have any social media. Maybe you are better off without these things dominating your life. Liam's obsession with the grain technology could be read as a social media type addiction. Though Charlie Brooker doesn't especially like the reduction of Black Mirror to a 'technology is bad' show and says that wasn't the intention (Brooker is fond of technology himself and follows new developments) in some of these Black Mirror stories technology clearly IS bad and out of control. And this sometimes mirrors our own reality. Technology has its positives and negatives.

The 'first season' of Black Mirror - if we can call three episodes a season - is exceptionally strong and doesn't have a single weak episode. All three episodes are interesting, well made and - most importantly - different. All of these episodes do their own thing but still feel like blood relatives to one another. They all feel like Black Mirror. The fans or critics who feel that Black Mirror was never the same or as good when it went to Netflix and had bigger budgets and American episodes would point to this first season as evidence. That was the show at its best they might argue. Those were the halcyon days before you got bigger budgets and episodes set in America and the show became more mainstream and even sentimental on occasion. The view that Black Mirror was better when it was a Channel 4 show is one that seems to irritate Charlie Brooker but it is a view that one can make a case for. This is of course not to say that Black Mirror didn't have any terrific episodes when it moved to Netflix because it clearly did. It does have two distinct eras though - Channel 4 and Netflix. The Channel 4 years for many constituted the best of the show - the undiluted version of Black Mirror at its darkest and sharpest.

SERIES 2 (2013)

BE RIGHT BACK

(Directed by Owen Harris, Written by Charlie Brooker)

SYNOPSIS - Martha (Hayley Atwell) and Ash (Domhnall Gleeson) are a happy young couple who move into a quiet country cottage together. Tragedy strikes though when Ash is killed in a car accident. Martha's friend Sarah (Sinead Matthews) tells Martha about a new AI service that might help mitigate some of the immense grief and loneliness she is feeling. The AI service collects all electronic data left by a deceased loved one and then through the mass of data impersonates that person through emails, messages and even phone conversations. Despite her initial reluctance to use the service, Martha is soon in constant communication with this AI version of her late boyfriend. But will she be willing to take the next step and have the AI downloaded into a synthetic body which looks exactly like Ash?

REVIEW - Be Right Back, like The Entire History of You, is another story about a relationship in which technology plays a prominent part. Unlike the grain implants in The Entire History of You, the AI impersonating a dead person through messaging in Be Right Back feels alarmingly plausible. In fact, this sort of thing has already happened in reality. The only plunge into science fiction comes when Martha is basically given an android version of her late boyfriend - which is obviously something we can't do yet in reality but may do in the far future. Charlie Brooker said this episode was inspired by him having to face the problem of whether or not to delete the phone contacts and messages of a friend who had died. It made him wonder whether the digital footprint left by a deceased person could be used by an artificial intelligence to make it seem as if that person was still alive and sending you messages and even talking to you on the phone. This part of the AI is so convincing that Martha feels as if she is contact with Ash from beyond the grave (which might, one could argue, make Be Right Back a sort of ghost story too). When she is contact with the AI version of Ash through messaging and phone calls it feels as if she is talking with the real Ash. Martha can't let go just yet. She isn't ready to move on so clings to this artificial whisper of Ash as if it is the real thing.

The real problems arise when the AI recreation of Ash is placed in a synthetic body. Martha soon begins to realise that while the AI can do a good impression of replicating a text or email Ash might send it can't possibly replicate all the quirks and flaws that make someone human. So in the end she comes to resent this synthetic version of Ash because it can never replace the real Ash. It is an impostor impersonating Ash. Martha begins to find the android AI version of Ash creepy and annoying in the end so you could say Be Right Back has some vague allusions to Pet Sematary. Ash is sort of back but he isn't really back. He's not the same. Be Right Back also has some parallels with the 1984 John Carpenter film Starman. In that film Jeff Bridges plays an alien who impersonates the late husband of Karen Allen's character. The AI synthetic version of Ash is doing something similar. The AI is impersonating Ash based on data and looks like Ash but ultimately finds it impossible to replicate all the little things - both good and bad - that make someone human. The AI is advanced in Be Right Back because it can even do jokes and humour. Our own real ChatGPT, by contrast, is not exactly S. J. Perelman.

Be Right Back has some similarities with Alfred Hitchcock's Vertigo in that a person becomes obsessed with recreating the image of a lost loved one. Be Right Back is really about grief and the difficulty of accepting what has happened. Another film which Be Right Back appears to be partly influenced by is Solaris. Solaris is a science fiction film directed by Andrei Tarkovsky based on the novel of the same name by Stanisław Lem. The film follows the story of a psychologist named Kris Kelvin (Donatas Banionis) who is sent to a space station orbiting the planet Solaris to investigate the strange behaviour of the crew members. Upon his arrival, Kelvin begins to experience bizarre and surreal events that challenge his perception of reality. Not least of which is the sudden appearance of his wife Hari (Natalya Bondarchuk) on the station. Hari died ten years ago on Earth. At the heart of the film lies the haunting relationship between Kris and Hari, whose interactions serve as a prism through which Tarkovsky explores themes of love, grief, and the nature of human connection. As Kris grapples with the enigmatic manifestations of Hari and his own inner turmoil, Solaris unfolds as a profound treatise on the complexities of memory and the ways in which we construct our identities through our relationships with others. Be Right Back explores similar themes.

Be Right Back is both touching and depressing at the same

time. This is a bleak slow burn sort of episode that gains a big boost by the strong performances of (especially) Hayley Atwell and Domhnall Gleeson. The themes of this story makes us question whether we might do the same in Martha's position. Would we use the AI in an attempt to spend more time with a deceased love one? We'd like to think that we wouldn't and would prefer to get by on happy memories but the temptation would definitely be there. Charlie Brooker said that when he wrote Be Right Back he had just become a father and this made him 'soppier' and more thoughtful in some of his writing. One can see a progression here in the writing away from the shock value of The National Anthem (a story which, though well played, betrays traces of the juvenile Brooker humour from his days on Oink! and writing occasionally offensive articles in video game magazines). What makes Be Right Back powerful is that Martha, consumed by grief, becomes vulnerable enough to go all in on his AI technology but then comes to realise that she's simply been fooling herself and Ash is gone. Martha would have been better off if she'd simply ignored the option of an AI Ash to talk to. Though it could mimic Ash it wasn't really him. The real Ash lives on in her memories - not in an AI computer programme.

Martha eventually decides to stuff the android version of Ash in the attic. The episode had pointedly begun with Ash saying that his mother moved photographs of loved ones in the attic when they died. She didn't want those reminders in plain sight because it was too painful. Martha has had a daughter by now (it was Ash's child) and allows the child to visit this strange shadow of Ash in the attic now and again. If one had a criticism of Be Right Back it would be that the scenes where Martha investigates the AI technology and begins to communicate with the AI version of Ash are more compelling than the scenes with the android Ash later on because they have more mystery and are more chillingly plausible. The stuff with the android Ash in the third act unavoidably treads more familiar (and fantastical ground too because while we have AI we can talk to we obviously don't have lifelike androids in real life) ground and the script doesn't really know what to do with the synthetic Ash once he is introduced into the story. So the story now becomes more derivative than what came before because a story about an android who looks human but can never master the fine details of being human is not exactly original in science fiction. It has been done a billion times from Data in Star Trek to the Roger Corman film Android to that terrible Robin Williams film and so on.

Martha comes to realise she has been the victim of a grief induced delusion. Technology can never replicate or bring back Ash. She must learn to live with the fact he is gone and move on with her life. The artificial version of Ash becomes like an old photograph moved to an out of the way place. A poignant and bittersweet reminder of happier times. Be Right Back generally tends to rank quite highly when people do their lists of Black Mirror episodes and you can see why. It is well directed, has a great central performance by Hayley Atwell and for the most part is generally plausible despite the science fiction trappings at the end. Martha's experience may well be a taste of what is to come in our own far flung future. If realistic artificial people ever become a thing it doesn't seem far-fetched at all to think that people might start marrying them or even trying to fashion them after lost loved ones. Who knows where it will all end?

WHITE BEAR

(Directed by Carl Tibbetts, Written by Charlie Brooker)

SYNOPSIS - A young woman (played by Lenora Crichlow) wakes up in a house with amnesia. She has no memory of who she is or even where she is. The television screen displays a strange bear symbol. The woman notices photographs of a man and a young girl in the house. She takes a photograph of the young girl - presuming perhaps that this might be a daughter or relative. Once outside, the woman discovers that society seems to be a dangerous and lawless place. Gangs of mysterious figures are prone to attack at any time. There are also placid onlookers who simply stand and film the attacks on their phones. The woman meets Jem (Tuppence Middleton) - who is some sort of resistance fighter. Jem explains that the strange signal turns people into voyeurs who film violence for entertainment. The main danger are the 'hunters' who (as the name implies) hunt humans. The amnesia ridden young woman becomes involved in a mission to destroy the transmitter broadcasting the television signal. But things are not as they seem in this world - as she will eventually find ...

REVIEW - White Bear is generally regarded to be one of the most celebrated not just of the early episodes of Black Mirror but of any era. White Bear is the sort of episode that is hard to live up to or repeat. it is just its own unique thing with a shocking twist the show struggled to ever match again. This story takes a more overt swing into horror and then pulls the rug out at the end with the Twilight Zone style twist. The start of White Bear plays somewhat like The Running Man, Mad Max or a zombie film - only in charmingly mundane English locations. It's an apocalyptic story where you assume the theme is how people have become desensitised to violence - to the point where they regard it as mindless entertainment to be filmed rather than something which should be stopped or reported. I gather this script went through two or three phases before the big twist was conjured so perhaps in the early drafts White Bear was more this type of straight ahead lawless dystopia story. It probably would have worked fine like that but the twist takes it to the next level as far as mean-spirited Black Mirror DNA goes. White Bear has a similar sort of template to the series three episode Shut Up and Dance in that we have a sympathetic central 'hero' who then turns out to be hiding a terrible secret which suddenly turns the character upside down and makes us look at them in a completely different light. That person we've been following through the story in White Bear? Well, it turns out they aren't the person we thought they were. They do say that monsters hide in plain sight.

The anthology television connoisseur may notice a number of antecedents in this episode. The oblivious onlookers evoke the people who gather around car crash aftermaths in The Crowd episode of Ray Bradbury Theater. The strange symbol evokes the Child's Play episode of Hammer House of Mystery & Suspense - where a family trapped in their house keep finding a symbol everywhere. The nightmare loop of the Lenora Crichlow's character evokes Carl Lanser - the man forced to relive a sea tragedy over and over again in the Twilight Zone episode Judgment Night. The nature of the predicament the young woman wakes to in White Bear also rather evokes the Twilight Zone story Five Characters in Search of an Exit - where five strangers find themselves trapped together in a metal cylinder with no memory of how they got there. The ever reliable Michael Smiley turns up in this episode as a contact of Jem who turns out to be a hunter who has double-crossed them. White Bear feels like an exploitation survival horror film in some of these sections and works well enough in this vein. Just as you think you've got this episode sussed though it spins off in another direction altogether. You definitely can't accuse White Bear of having a story that is easy to predict.

The big twist in White Bear arrives when the young woman with amnesia attempts to complete her mission to destroy the transmitter. A gun she was given only fires harmless confetti. It's a dud. A fake gun. What is going on? Smiley's character Baxter, who was apparently killed by Jem, is suddenly alive. His death was faked. They are all now in a television studio with an audience. Baxter is the ringmaster and Jem is merely an actress. Everything we've just watched was fake and staged. It was all an elaborate ruse. It transpires that the young amnesiac woman is named Victoria Skillane. Victoria is a notorious criminal figure. Along with her boyfriend (who hung himself in prison) she abducted and murdered a little girl named Jemima. Jemima had a toy white bear and this became a symbol of the tragic search for her. Victoria is put in a glass box and taken back to the house where this story began as people jeer and barrack her. Victoria's punishment is to relive this scenario over and over again. Her memory is wiped each day - in a painful way with electrodes. This is the White Bear Justice Park and there'll be escape or respite for Victoria.

The twist in White Bear is bleak in the best Black Mirror tradition. We are now forced to completely rethink our attitude to the sympathetic and frightened young woman who was the central character in this story. We are also forced to react to her unusual punishment. Does she deserve the horrible fate this society has decided for her? An endless loop of punishment and misery? The most obvious true crime parallel to Victoria here would appear to be Myra Hindley. Hindley was a typist who fell under the spell of the vile Ian Brady. The crimes he committed with Myra Hindley shocked and appalled Britain in the 1960s. Brady murdered children and recorded their pleas for mercy. Hindley was an accomplice in these awful crimes. Capital punishment had only recently been abolished in Britain so Brady had a close shave when it came to avoiding a death sentence. Most people at the time probably would have been delighted to see Ian Brady hung for his crimes. Myra Hindley would later blame Brady for the murders and said that she was fearful of him and abused. Despite her expressions of remorse and attempts to get parole, few really believed that Hindley was innocent or an unwilling accomplice and she will probably forever remain the most infamous female figure in British true crime history.

There were attempts, especially by Lord Longford, to release Myra Hindley from prison but the newspapers and public were appalled by this. Hindley died in prison in 2002. Myra Hindley was still so despised that when she died the prison authorities struggled to find an undertaker willing to handle the cremation. Victoria Skillane is basically then revealed to be an analogue of Myra Hindley in Black Mirror. There is no one in society more despised than someone who harmed or killed a child. Many people would happily see the death penalty used or brought back for such crimes. White Bear, without explicitly taking a side, does force us though to question the ethics of Victoria's treatment. Might she have genuine remorse? Could she be rehabilitated? Is it right to torture someone - even if they have perpetrated the most heinous crime? If her memory is constantly wiped doesn't this pose an ethical and moral problem because Victoria Skillane is now being endlessly punished for a crime she has no idea she even committed. So we feel conflicted and uncomfortable at the resolution and these are emotions that Black Mirror, at its best, is able to make the audience feel. This is one of those episodes which lingers in the memory for a while after it ends.

The story in White Bear touches upon a number of real life cases and not just Hindley. Maxine Carr was the young woman who was living with Ian Huntley when he murdered two girls in Soham. Carr, though not involved in the actual crimes, did provide Huntley with a false alibi in an attempt to help him out. After a short prison sentence Carr had to have her name changed and go into hiding because of threats from the public. The character of Victoria, you might venture, is a sort of mash-up of Hindley and Carr. She was a useful idiot for a child killer and maybe a lot worse than that too. Despite the gravity of her crimes we are uncomfortable with the treatment of Victoria Skillane at the end of this episode. She is essentially being tortured. It doesn't feel right. And turning justice into a grim reality television type spectacle is not dignified nor tasteful. Mob justice is not a good prescription for society because, as Rod Serling famously said on The Twilight Zone, for civilisation to survive the human race has to remain civilised. White Bear is one of the most memorable Black Mirror episodes with a kicker of a twist. It is another solid brick in the largely excellent Channel 4 era of the show.

THE WALDO MOMENT

(Directed by Bryn Higgins, Written by Charlie Brooker)

SYNOPSIS - Jamie Salter (Daniel Rigby) is a comedian who is the voice and actor behind an animated cartoon bear named Waldo. As something of a publicity gimmick, Waldo the Bear stands as a candidate at a by-election. Waldo seems to be doing surprisingly well in the election but Jamie - the real person behind Waldo - is not really cut out for politics and soon becomes unhappy with this charade. Jamie's brush with the world of politics leaves him deeply unimpressed with the people put up for election. He also learns the hard way that Waldo is the star and he is expendable...

REVIEW - The Waldo Moment tends to rank fairly low when it comes to Black Mirror lists and it isn't too hard to see why although this episode isn't as bad as some made it out to be. Charlie Brooker expressed some dissatisfaction with this episode and said he didn't have sufficient time to work on the script. The general idea for this story was one that Brooker and Chris Morris came up with while they were working on Nathan Barley. Nathan Barley was a short lived but cultish Channel 4 comedy show which both predicted and skewered the rise of the hipsters. The Waldo Moment feels a lot like some half-baked idea leftover from Nathan Barley or some political comedy satire miniseries that Brooker never got around to making. It is an awkward fit for Black Mirror and one is never entirely convinced that this story belongs in the show. The two main problems with The Waldo Moment is that the satire often feels vague and obvious and also that this doesn't even feel much like an episode of Black Mirror in the end. The bleak ending where Jamie is a down and out and the political system has become totalitarian feels like a tacked on afterthought and seems as if it comes out of the blue.

One other problem with The Waldo Moment is that the central idea is not exactly original because we have seen it happen in real life. Comedy, celebrity or publicity gimmick candidates standing in elections has happened for real in many nations. Occasionally they even get elected. The main problem is that The Waldo Moment just about works as a modestly diverting political black comedy in its own right but judged as an episode of Black Mirror it feels out of place and falls some way short of the high standard that has already been set by episodes like White Bear and Fifteen Million Merits. Charlie Brooker has said that Boris Johnson was the salient influence on this story. Johnson is Waldo the Bear going all the way to Downing Street. There was something grimly inevitable about Johnson ending up as the prime minster one day. He'd probably been plotting this since he was at some toff festooned prep school. In his imagination Boris Johnson probably imagines himself to be Winston Churchill. He's a strangely odd character who matches a decent wit (even his critics would have to concede that Boris Johnson has a sense of humour) with a weird form of political autism and shameless spivvery.

Take that election for example when all the leaders gamely got their traditional battering at the hands of the forensic Andrew Neil. Johnson, deducing that he was ahead in the polls, simply waited until everyone else had taken their turn with Neil and then bailed out of his own interview! The Andrew Neil evasion was symbolic of the lack of honour and shame in Boris Johnson. This is a man who would literally do anything to get elected. It is often suggested that Boris Johnson, so prominent in Vote Leave during the referendum, didn't actually believe in quitting the EU and only joined the leave camp for personal political reasons. Johnson, this theory goes, judged that remain would win a narrow vote and that he - as the most famous leaver - would see his position in his party greatly strengthened (because the rank and file of the Conservative Party have always loathed the EU). Knowing Boris Johnson as we do it wouldn't surprise you in the slightest if this theory was the truth. Johnson seemed to have some appeal for working-class voters who had turned on the Labour Party but can you imagine what Johnson really thinks about working-class people in private?

Johnson has always been a dreadful chancer and bungler. This is a man who makes things up as he goes along. Boris Johnson is a joke that stopped being funny years ago. The stupid haircut, Latin quips, stooped walk. So in the grand scheme of things - where Boris Johnson can become prime minister - a cartoon bear having a shot of winning a by-election maybe isn't such a stretch. Stranger Things have probably happened. One of the reasons why Donald Trump was so successful in politics is that he came into it off the back of fronting a popular reality television show. You could sort of say that Trump is Waldo the Bear writ large. A problem with The Waldo Moment is that Waldo the Bear isn't a charismatic or funny enough creation to make us credibly believe he has become this big comedy sensation. The humour in this episode is rather crude and juvenile at times - harking back to some of the worst instincts of early Brooker. The Waldo Moment feels like a step backwards after the likes of The Entire History of You and White Bear. This is the only minor dud in the Channel 4 era of the show.

One of the obvious problems with this episode is that it feels jarring to go from these science fiction dystopia stories into a dark political comedy satire. The Waldo Moment feels as if it is stretching and even ignoring the general perception of what constitutes the Black Mirror remit. The technology theme is represented by Waldo himself but this theme isn't very interesting compared to the strange screen dominated world of Fifteen Million Merits or the AI Ash talking to Martha in Be Right Back.

Jamie Salter as a protagonist in The Waldo Moment is uncharismatic and unsympathetic and we struggle to believe that the Labour candidate Gwendolyn Harris (Chloe Pirrie) would really develop any romantic interest in him. Not to say that this episode is a complete waste of time though. Tobias Menzies is good as the Tory candidate Liam Monroe (one of the best scenes comes at a debate where Monroe reels off a load of facts about the man behind Waldo) and the script does a good job in skewering the cynical and careerist nature of politics. Gwendolyn is well aware she can't win this by-election but her campaign in necessary to build a CV that might nab her a more winnable seat in the future. Most people will have experienced some useless careerist politician being parachuted into their region with no knowledge or interest in that area but simply using it as a means to climb the greasy pole. Gwendolyn Harris is that sort of politician - though perhaps more decent than some others in her grubby field. So the script here is slightly more nuanced than you might expect and skewers all sides when it comes to politics. Brooker even skewers, to a degree, comedians and celebrities who thrust themselves into politics with only a superficial knowledge of the subjects they are now pompously professing to suddenly be experts in.

The moral of the story is that politics is too serious to treat as a joke comedy gimmick or simply a career for some egomaniac or toff who believes it is their divine right to rule. The Waldo Moment doesn't give us the answers but it does pose some questions about the system. Are the right people going into politics? Why do our elected representatives frequently turn out to be so inept and useless? Another theme here is Jamie losing control of the Waldo character and having it taken away from him. The people who own Waldo don't need Jamie Salter. They can just hire someone else. This basically ruins Jamie's life if the ending is anything to go by. When you take away Waldo the Bear who is Jamie and does he have anything to offer? It could be the case that Jamie was using Waldo as a mask to hide behind. The fictitious cartoon bear turns out to be of more value than Jamie. Jamie is expendable but the bear isn't. The Waldo Moment is by no means a terrible episode of television but it does plainly suffer from not feeling very much like a Black Mirror story and while watchable is not really something that lodges in the memory for long afterwards in the way that the very best episodes of Black Mirror tend to do. So on the whole then this episode feels weakish and slightly atypical when set aside the other Channel 4 stories. It doesn't feel like an essential watch in the way things like White Bear and White Christmas do.

2014 SPECIAL

WHITE CHRISTMAS

(Directed by Carl Tibbetts, Written by Charlie Brooker)

SYNOPSIS - Joe Potter (Rafe Spall) and Matt Trent (Jon Hamm) live together in an isolated cabin at Christmas. They appear to have been here for some years as a form of punishment but the actual details seem to be vague to both men. Matt decides to cook some dinner and get Joe talking. Joe isn't too chatty though so Matt has to talk about himself first in order to get Joe's confidence. Matt tells two stories about himself before Joe is ready to talk about his own life. These two men are both sitting on dark secrets and it's all about to come out...

REVIEW - This was the last Channel 4 episode before the show moved to Netflix. Channel 4 hadn't been very happy with the scripts for a proposed series three so did not commission one but they did consent to a Christmas special. Charlie Brooker feared at the time that White Christmas would be the last ever Black Mirror so he laced it with some references to past episodes. This episode is sort of like a horror anthology film in the way we see three stories and have the framing device (or wraparound if you prefer) of the two men talking in the cottage. A particular influence on White Christmas was Dead of Night. Dead of Night is a classic 1945 Ealing Studios portmanteau horror film featuring stories directed by Alberto Cavalcanti, Charles Crichton, Basil Dearden and Robert Hamer. This is - above all - the film that Amicus used as their touchstone when they made their own series of horror anthologies in the sixties and seventies. Dead of Night begins with architect Walter Craig (Mervyn Johns) arriving at a country house where other guests are waiting. Walter experiences a strange sense of deja vu and believes this has happened before. Dead of Night is the Citizen Kane of anthology horror films and hugely influential in that subgenre of horror.

Jon Hamm ended up in this episode because he was a fan of Black Mirror and asked to meet Charlie Brooker while he was in Britain. Mad Men was still running at the time so it was something of a coup for Black Mirror to get a big star like this. Hamm is not exactly stretched too much in White Christmas playing a charming but heartless rogue but he's very good in this episode. White Christmas has an excellent cast all round because Rafe Spall is equally good as Joe Potter and Game of Thrones stars Oona Chaplin and Natalia Tena both make their mark in smaller parts. White Christmas happily ticks a number of boxes in that it is a Christmas episode, a compendium and quintessentially Black Mirror. As a last hurrah for the Channel 4 iteration of the show it is hard to think of a better way to go out than White Christmas. It transpires in the White Christmas flashbacks that Matt Trent was something of a grifter and worked in technology. A device known as Z-eyes is implanted in people in this near future society. This technology records one's interactions and the feed can be watched by others. It's the sort of vaguely sci-fi technology we see in numerous Black Mirror episodes and a device that serves the plot.

Trent set himself up as a dating guru who coaches men online in how to be more confident and successful with women. However, it all went tragically wrong when a young client named Harry (Rasmus Hardiker) was murdered by a troubled woman named Jennifer (Natalia Tena) during a live 'coaching' session Trent was conducting and others were watching as entertainment. This sequence is very well done and builds a creeping sense of doom as it slowly becomes apparent that Harry might be in danger. The reaction of Trent to the tragedy is to close his computer and presumably try to mask anything linking him to this murder. Trent is charming at first glance but we see he is not the sort of person to take responsibility for his actions. He is the sort of person you would trust at your peril. Perhaps the most disturbing part of the episode comes when we see another of Trent's past jobs. He was involved in training 'cookies'. In this society rich people can create a little 'cookie' clone of themselves which lives in an egg and must act as a personal technology slave running the house and its systems. The general idea is that the cookie has one's memories and personality so will know exactly what you like and how the house should be run. This is very convenient for the real person but not so nice for the 'cookie' that has been created as a slave.

A woman named Greta (Oona Chaplin) creates an identical 'cookie' of herself to this end but the cookie is not too keen on being a slave. This is where Trent comes in. He has the ability to speed up time for the cookie - making them experience months of tedium and stress in an instant. So he's basically torturing the cookie to make it compliant and do as it is told. What makes this scenario terrifying is that the cookie believes itself to be a person but then must deal with the horrifying realisation it is just a little piece of imprisoned technology created to be a slave. It can never be a real person - despite being a thinking sentient duplicate of an actual person. These scenes make White Christmas one of the darkest Black Mirror stories but things will get darker still before the end. For those who think Black Mirror was at its best when it was bleak and

British, well, White Christmas will give you exactly what you are looking for. You could argue that this is the among the most essential episodes of Black Mirror in the way it explores the themes most associated with the show and does so in a darkly memorable and unforgettable sort of way.

Joe Potter, initially reticent and aloof, eventually starts to talk about his past in the cottage. His tale will represent the third story in this anthology. It's to the credit of this episode that the story uses the expanded 74 minute running time to its advantage and doesn't feel padded in the slightest. The framing device in the cabin works well and is incorporated into the overall story in a clever way. We learn that Joe had a fiancée named Beth (Janet Montgomery) and they were once happy but things quickly turned sour when she became pregnant. Joe was delighted at the pregnancy but then mortified and angered when Beth told him she didn't want the baby. This dispute caused the couple to break up but it assuredly wasn't what Joe wanted. In the end Beth used the Z-eyes technology to 'block' Joe. This meant that they only appeared to one another as a fuzzy blurred outline and could no longer speak to each other. It's like when you block someone on social media or on a forum - only this time you've blocked someone in the real physical world! Joe now becomes a stalker. He is aware that Beth went through with the pregnancy and had a daughter. So he is consumed by the knowledge he has a daughter but the mother doesn't want anything to do with him. Joe now devotes his time to tracking them down and spying on them.

Joe tracks Beth down to an isolated cottage but when he tries to talk to the child and sees it up close for the first time it is obvious this isn't his biological daughter. Beth was having an affair when she became pregnant. That's why she couldn't face Joe and didn't want him to see the child. Beth's father is in the cabin looking after the child and when the grandfather confronts Joe the frazzled Joe beats him to death with a snow globe and runs away. The child was left alone in the house and wandered outside in the snow where it died of cold and hunger. So once again early Black Mirror is as bleak as it can get. It transpires that Joe and Trent are not in a cottage but one of the cookie eggs we saw Greta in earlier. Trent (who was arrested) was simply trying to get Joe to confess to murder for the police. So this was a plea-bargain deal. If he could make Joe confess he would get off with a lighter punishment for his own crimes. His task accomplished Trent is set free but as punishment for the young man who was murdered taking part in Trent's romantic coaching session, Trent is 'blocked' forever by the Z-eyes and no one can see him.

This detail rather evokes a 1986 episode of the 'new' Twilight Zone called To See the Invisible Man. To See the Invisible Man takes place in some regimented Orwellian future society where people are punished for not being 'social' by having a mark placed on their head which marks them as an 'invisible'. If you are an 'invisible' no one is allowed to speak to you or even acknowledge your presence. Joe, meanwhile, has a fate worse than death in the cookie. A rather cruel police officer adjusts the cookie controls so he experiences 1,000 years per minute with Wizzard's I Wish It Could Be Christmas Every Day blasting away. White Christmas is mean spirited to be sure but this deliciously dark quality makes it all the more compelling. This is a fine stab at an anthology (within an anthology!) story with a top notch cast. White Christmas marks the end of an era because it was the last Channel 4 produced Black Mirror. The show thereafter moved to Netflix where - with a few notable exceptions - it was never quite as dark and bleak again. There would now be regular episodes set in America with American casts and a clear attempt to be more mainstream and branch out with different types of stories. Did Black Mirror lose its edge with the move to Netflix? Did it diminish the show in the end? Well, let's find out as we now move to the Netflix era of Black Mirror.

SERIES 3 (2016)

NOSEDIVE

(Directed by Joe Wright, Written by Charlie Brooker, Teleplay by: Rashida Jones & Mike Schur)

SYNOPSIS - Nosedive takes place in a world where implants log every interaction. You are encouraged to instantly rate everything - sort of like social media likes or online user reviews. The amount of positive comments or good reviews you accrue in return determines your socioeconomic status in society. A woman Lacie Pound (Bryce Dallas Howard) wants to improve her rating in order to acquire a nicer apartment. So she's basically having to suck up to everyone and be false and fake in order to boost her popularity. Lacie is delighted to be chosen as the maid of honour at the wedding of childhood friend Naomi (Alice Eve). Naomi and her swanky friends have a higher social status than Lacie and so Lacie thinks this wedding will be the perfect place to pick up many positive 'reviews' and boost her own rating. However, things do not quite according to plan...

REVIEW - Nosedive was the first episode of Black Mirror after the move to Netflix and it does feel very different from the Channel 4 years. The budget is bigger, the story is set in the United States and the tone is more comedic and lightweight than we are used to. The (rather obvious) theme of this episode is the shallow and superficial pastime of chasing online popularity. You'd be much better off if you just ignored all that stuff and didn't bother playing the game. In the society depicted in Nosedive though such matters are inextricably tied into your status in society. If you want the nicer things in life you are going to have to suck up to the people and services you encounter - even if you don't care for them very much. Lacie is determined to play the game and have nice things so must wander through life like one of those smiling tabula rasa androids in The Stepford Wives giving fake compliments to people who couldn't less what happens to her. It's like the lyrics in that Smiths song. In my life, why do I give valuable time, To people who don't care if I live or die? The society is Nosedive is a place where reviews and opinions are almost meaningless because everyone is sucking up to others to get a good rating in return. Few people are being honest. It is a society built on being false and dishonest.

So the society in this episode is nightmarish indeed because it is forcing people to be fake, lie, and act like grinning robots. And what sort of society heaps economic and social status on people who get the most likes for a picture of their lunch? A society that has gone mad indeed. Nosedive is laced then with commentary on the vanity and superficiality of the online world. All these egomaniacs endlessly taking photographs of themselves and posting pictures of their lunch. The biggest influence on this episode appears to be the John Hughes film Planes, Trains and Automobiles - where Steve Martin's uptight advertising executive tries to get home for Thanksgiving but ends up on the road trip from hell with John Candy's slobbish salesman. Lacie's journey to the wedding also turns into a comical road trip disaster where everything that can go wrong does go wrong. She can't get on a flight, can only rent a terrible car, and ends up hitch-hiking and tagging a lift from a trucker. Lacie's 'rating' plummets ever downwards during this trip and she ends up a bedraggled and frazzled mess by the time she arrives at the wedding. This episode then has a broadly comedic tone. It becomes a road trip farce sort of story.

By now, Naomi doesn't even want Lacie at the wedding anymore but Lacie sneaks in and delivers an uncomfortable speech before threatening to destroy the rag-doll she and Naomi made as children. The pressure of having to maintain a fake personality has finally made Lacie snap. She is exhausted.

Lacie ends up in a police cell and her rating implants are removed. A man in another cell (played by Sope Dirisu) and Lacie dispense comical insults at one another. They no longer have to pretend to like everything and everyone. They are no longer being rated in return. So for the first time in the episode Lacie is truly happy. She can just say whatever she wants. All that nonsense where she has to be fake and pretend to like everyone is out the window. So this episode has a happy ending - something which Netflix Black Mirror does more often than the Channel 4 version (in fact, it is hard to think of a crystal clear happy ending in the Channel 4 episodes). Nosedive is generally amusing and watchable and Bryce Dallas Howard is terrific as the lead. Compared to things like White Bear, Fifteen Million Merits and White Christmas it doesn't always feel much like a Black Mirror episode though. There is definitely an adjustment needed on the part of the viewer to get used to this slicker and at times more generic version of the show. The rough edges of the early episodes are no longer so evident and this unavoidably means a loss of some of that early Black Mirror DNA. Nosedive ultimately feels a trifle mainstream and obvious compared to earlier Black Mirror episodes and the longer running time is not necessarily to the benefit of the story.

The artificial look of this episode with the pastel colours is nicely done and appropriately superficial for the themes of the story. Nosedive is fine for what it is but does feel middling and lightweight compared to the best Black Mirror episodes and doesn't have much of a punch. The supporting cast is good - Cherry Jones in particular as a trucker named Susan who gives Lacie a lift and has no interest in playing the popularity game to get on in society. The last straw for Susan was when her late husband was refused cancer medication because he didn't have a high enough 'rating'. So not playing the popularity game in this society has serious ramifications - which merely compounds how insane the whole thing is in the first place. We see that Lacie's brother (played by James Norton) is also uninterested in the vapid popularity contest this society has turned life into. Those who reject the modus operandi of this society tend to be the happiest. They are free to just be themselves. Nosedive therefore has a positive message that integrity and being true to oneself is more important than money. It's a lesson that Lacie must learn over the course of the story.

The plot of Nosedive is similar to an episode of Community which had a similar theme but Charlie Brooker has said he was unaware of Community when he wrote Nosedive. Though the plot of Nosedive might sound like a near future nightmare something similar was actually tried in China in the form of the Social Credit System. This system logged a number of factors like online posts and behaviour, financial prudence, timekeeping and social conduct and then gave businesses and individuals a trust rating which affected things like their ability to take out loans or even travel. So maybe the plot of Nosedive isn't fiction at all! It could be the case that in the future our lifestyle and access to services will be influenced by our online popularity rating. A terrifying thought indeed.

Nosedive feels like Black Mirror spreading its wings with the bigger budget and longer format. This is a slick and great looking episode that - with its road trip shenanigans - leans more into comedy and farce than a lot of the early episodes. It's a solid episode and very watchable but probably not something you would place anywhere near the Black Mirror top table. In a sense Nosedive (and The Waldo Moment) are true to the anthology format because though somewhat atypical the idea of an anthology show is one is never quite sure what sort of story you are going to get from week to week. This is true of The Twilight Zone and Tales of the Unexpected and it is now true of Black Mirror. With this episode Charlie Brooker has made it clear that going forward not every episode of Black Mirror will be a grimdark bleak dystopia.

PLAYTEST

(Directed by Dan Trachtenberg, Written by Charlie Brooker)

SYNOPSIS - A young American named Cooper (Wyatt Russell) goes backpacking abroad to escape from the grief of his father dying with Alzheimer's disease. While in London, he crashes with a tech journalist named Sonja (Hannah John-Kamen) and runs out of money thanks to fraud. He learns of an opportunity to make some money though testing a new video game for a company boss named Shou (Ken Yamamura). The game requires implants in the back of his neck and places him in a virtual reality scenario where he must survive a night in a spooky house. This game is exceptionally real though and Cooper is about to have a very rough and challenging night indeed...

REVIEW - Playtest, if you strip away the technology theme, is basically a haunted house episode but a pretty solid haunted house story as far as they go. This is one of those Black Mirror episodes that seemed to get a better reception from fans than critics and the last time I looked it has a healthy 8 out of 10 rating on IMDB. This episode runs to 57 minutes and the longer running time of Netflix era Black Mirror can make some of these tales a trifle draggy (Rod Serling's Twilight Zone - the fourth season aside - was in and out in half an hour with no problem) but Playtest is generally entertaining throughout and never threatens to outstay its welcome too much. You can really see the increased budget in this episode with the elaborate and inventive special effects on show. There isn't an awful lot in this episode when it comes to plot or character development but it does what it says on the tin and gives you a horror themed Black Mirror episode with technology at the core of the story. Video games in Black Mirror stories are a recurring theme because Charlie Brooker used to write for a video game magazine in the 1990s - which was perhaps the most exciting and interesting time to follow video games. Brooker would have experienced that massive quantum leap in the early 1990s when Doom came out and astonished everyone.

Dan Trachtenberg, the director of this episode, would later go on to resurrect the ailing Predator franchise with Prey. He also directed the interesting thriller film 10 Cloverfield Lane. So this Black Mirror episode has excellent direction and special effects and plenty of atmosphere. But is the atmosphere strong enough to mitigate the less than original premise of this episode? Well, by and large yes although the ending feels like a bit of a cop out and borrowed from An Occurrence at Owl Creek Bridge (Ambrose Bierce's short story). An Occurrence at Owl Creek Bridge has (spoiler warning) a twist ending where everything that has occurred turns out to be the daydream of a man in the seconds before he died. Playtest pulls the same trick. Playtest also has similarities with a Twilight Zone episode called Perchance to Dream. Perchance to Dream is about a man with a cardiac condition who tells his psychiatrist Dr Rathmann (John Larch) that if he falls asleep he thinks he will die. The reason? He has been trapped in a recurring dream that always features a sultry carnival dancer named Maya (Suzanne Lloyd) trying to entice him into a funfair and onto a roller coaster with the intention of frightening him to death. Perchance to Dream is notable for being the first Twilight Zone contribution by the great Charles Beaumont.

Playtest unavoidably owes something to the many haunted house films and television episodes made over the years like 1408 and the 1985 Steve Miner film House. Playtest also reminds one of A Question of Fear - an enjoyable segment in the Rod Serling fronted anthology show Night Gallery. A Question of Fear opens at an exclusive gentleman's club where Dr Mazi (Fritz Weaver) tells his friends about a terrifying experience he had at a house that is said to be haunted. Overhearing the conversation is the macho and arrogant

Colonel Denny Malloy (Leslie Nielsen). Malloy scoffs at all this talk of ghosts and haunted houses and says that he is personally incapable of fear. Mazi decides to take the Colonel at his word and says he will give him $15,000 if he spends a night at the haunted house alone. There are - as you would expect - a number of video game influences and Easter eggs in Playtest. A particular influence is obviously Resident Evil. Resident Evil, also known as Biohazard in Japan, is a survival horror video game developed and published by Capcom in 1996. The game, which is patently inspired by (among other things) the zombie films of George Romero, follows the story of S.T.A.R.S. members Chris Redfield and Jill Valentine as they investigate the mysterious mansion of the Umbrella Corporation in the outskirts of Raccoon City. In many ways, Resident Evil refines the mechanics of the horror game Alone in the Dark (which was rich in atmosphere but could be a bit slow and clunky).

You could argue that Playtest is the first Black Mirror episode which feels like a fairly undiluted horror story for most of its duration. While the premise of someone staying in a haunted house has been done to death this episode does at least have a slightly different approach in that the protagonist is playing a game so assumes nothing is real but then begins to have doubts about that and worry about his safety. The game Cooper is testing in Playtest is designed to find his fears. Though not explicitly stated as an influence this reminds one of the film Galaxy of Terror. Galaxy of Terror is a 1981 science fiction horror film produced by Roger Corman and directed by Bruce D Clark. The premise has a ship sent to the desolate planet of Morganthus to investigate what happened to another ship which crashed there. The crew of the Morganthus are dragged to the surface and have a most unpleasant experience when they start to be killed off by mysterious dark forces which seem to be able to tap into their darkest fears.

The spider-monster in Playtest with the face of a childhood

bully Cooper remembers is appropriately creepy and perhaps a nod to The Thing - which Wyatt Russell's real life father Kurt obviously starred in. Playtest attempts to be one step ahead of the viewer with the story and indeed the ending. it is revealed that Cooper died after less than a second in the game - killed by a phone call from his mother (he ignored the instructions to turn his phone off). So everything which occurred was simply a second of Cooper's life. The AI of the game made it seem much longer though and tormented him in his dying moments. This gives Playtest a predictable (and not exactly original) ending but a suitably dark twist all the same. What is equally dark is the company testing this dangerous tech on someone and then appearing unconcerned when the test subject died - almost as if this possibility was something they didn't consider impossible. The ending is quite poignant because Cooper is not some villain in an Amicus horror film getting his just desserts. He's actually a decent chap and doesn't deserve this horrible fate. The attempts to lace in fragments of Wyatt's past and his family in this episode come off as somewhat vague and underfleshed. The basic core of Playtest though, a horror caper set in a spooky mansion, is watchable enough.

Playtest is perfectly solid and decent for what it is but it isn't one of those Black Mirror episodes you remember too much about afterwards. You are entertained by Playtest but it doesn't stay in the memory for very long. It doesn't have the story depth and nuance of the very best episodes of the show and the dark twist at the end is not very original. This is just basically Black Mirror doing a haunted house episode - which is fine but not the show playing to its strengths because there are a million other places where you can get this sort of thing. The next episode would thankfully be a bit more novel and draw on the early DNA of the show a lot more than Nosedive and Playtest. Thus far then season three of Black Mirror has been solid but hasn't blown our socks off. Playtest is highly efficient and has some good moments but it isn't the sort of story that threatens to get anywhere near the best episodes of the Channel 4 years of the show. Those who were starting to worry about Netflix Black Mirror coming off as too generic and mainstream so far would be cheered by the next episode though - which is bleak, British and something of a throwback to the early days.

SHUT UP AND DANCE

(Directed by James Watkins, Written by Charlie Brooker)

SYNOPSIS - A meek teenage fast food employee named Kenny (Alex Lawther) who lives with his mother and sister has his laptop infected with malware and is told by hackers that they've used his webcam to get footage of him enjoying himself while watching porn. The mortified Kenny is told by the hackers that he must complete a series of tasks or this webcam footage will be released. These tasks eventually escalate into bank robbery and a fight to the death with another blackmailed victim. Kenny has to complete most of these tasks with Hector (Jerome Flynn) - another blackmailed man who the hackers know arranged to cheat on his wife at a hotel with a prostitute. What exactly do the hackers want and will Kenny and Hector manage to complete these various tasks in time?

REVIEW - Shut Up and Dance often tends to rank quite low on subjective Black Mirror critic lists but I've never quite understood why because this is one the best episodes of the show and pure Black Mirror - despite the absence of science fiction or fantasy. This is very much in the vein of the Channel 4 era with its British setting and nasty and bleak edge. The fact that Shut Up and Dance is rough around the edges with a grim story makes it refreshing in a season of Black Mirror where the show is suddenly slicker and more American than it used to be in the past. You feel like Shut Up and Dance could have slotted quite comfortably into one of the Channel 4 seasons of the show. The biggest influence on Shut Up and Dance would appear to be Die Hard with a Vengeance. In that film the villain forces John McClane and a civilian (played by Samuel L. Jackson) to race around New York solving puzzles and doing tasks in order to prevent bombs going off. Shut Up and Dance has a similar premise with Kenny and Hector having to carry out various task to precise deadlines - only in an English suburbia rather than New York!

The motivation of the characters in Shut Up and Dance is very different too because they are seeking to placate the hackers and stop the information the blackmailers have on them being released. The stakes seem much higher for Hector than Kenny at first glance because he has a wife and children. His marriage is at stake. But it turns out in the end that young Kenny is the one with even more to lose. It's a solid twist which completely subverts our previous assumptions about what we've just watched. Kenny, thanks to the (trademark) twitchy and nervous performance of Alex Lawther, is a very sympathetic character throughout most of Shut Up and Dance and serves as our window into the story. Kenny is something of an outsider and meek and mild. We see that Kenny is treated with disdain by the other (bigger) lads who work at the fast food place with him. Kenny's mother (played by Camilla Power) seems to dote on him and treat him like a child despite the fact he is in his late teens. There is still something of the child about Kenny - despite his age. He seems like a naïve innocent and so it is understandable that we feel for Kenny and root for him once he is plunged into this strange and unpleasant scenario by the hackers. We don't want anything bad to happen to Kenny because we rather like him and have sympathy for his plight.

Kenny's problems all stem from his sister borrowing his laptop while he is out at work. Kenny does not like his sister using his laptop - for reasons which eventually become evident at the end of the episode. Kenny puts a padlock on his door (to stop his sister using his computer) and discovers his laptop is infected with a virus due to his sister trying to watch a film through a website which obviously turned out to be unsafe. Kenny downloads an anti-malware to get rid of the virus but it turns out to be a bogus criminal one which gives hackers access to his computer. They contact Kenny and tell him they have footage from his webcam of Kenny enjoying some porn. He must now do as they say or they will make this footage public. Now, you might be thinking at this point that Kenny should just call their bluff and ignore them but he doesn't. The reason why he doesn't take this course of action only becomes clear at the end. Kenny is not in a position to take any chances - hence his desperation. Kenny is now terrified and willing to do literally anything the blackmailers say. He feigns illness to get off work and is now at the beck and call of the hackers.

Kenny is ordered to drive to a hotel where he meets a middle-aged man named Hector. Hector is also being blackmailed by the hackers. This chalk and cheese duo are then ordered to rob a bank - which provides a memorable and unusual bank robbery sequence because this bank looks more like a country post office than a bank and Kenny is wearing a ridiculous disguise and wets himself as he demands the money. Hector had insisted he'd be better as the getaway driver so it was poor Kenny who had to rob the bank. It's to the credit of Jerome Flynn that he doesn't make Hector a sleaze ball or villain or bully in this story. Hector is a flawed man to be sure but he's decent enough to Kenny in this bizarre situation they find themselves in. Shut Up and Dance rattles along at breakneck pace and maintains an unsettling atmosphere - which becomes darker still in the third act. Kenny's predicament is as scary as anything in more fantastical Black Mirror stories because it is plausible - or at least feels plausible. The idea of someone gaining control of your computer and trying to blackmail you is frightening. We become curious in this episode to know what exactly the hackers want. We see they have blackmailed a number of people in the episode for things like racism and infidelity.

So we start to wonder if there is a specific reason for this blackmailing spree besides the criminal impulse and amusement. Do these hackers see themselves as doing a service to society by targeting these people? There is a rather suspicious looking teenager loitering by the hotel desk when Kenny and Hector leave. Is he one of the hackers checking up on them? It is never confirmed or denied but it seems probable. Kenny and Hector are ordered to part company (Hector is told to junk the car they robbed the bank with) and Kenny is instructed to go into some woodland. He encounters a man in the woods and is told by the hackers they must fight to the death. A drone hovers above to capture everything. The man (played by Paul Bazely) is also being blackmailed due to his webcam becoming compromised. He asks Kenny how young the people in the porn he was watching were. The man was clearly watching child porn and the question hits a raw nerve for Kenny. Kenny doesn't answer the question. So now we think back to the scene in the fast food place earlier where Kenny handed the toy to the little girl as she left. Kenny seemed to linger on that moment of interaction longer than necessary as if it was the greatest thing that had ever happened to him. In hindsight that moment was weird. There was something slightly off about it.

So now it all falls into place. Kenny was watching child porn and it was clearly a regular thing for him. That's why he put a padlock on his door so his sister couldn't use his computer. That's why he was so terrified when his laptop was hacked. That's why he was willing to do literally anything to keep a lid on this dark secret. So, just as with White Bear, we have spent most of the story in sympathy with someone who turned out to be hiding a terrible dark secret. I gather some drafts of the Shut Up and Dance script didn't have this twist. There was also a draft where it was Hector and not Kenny was the one with the awful secret. The end is devastating because we liked Kenny and felt sorry for him. Now we have to rethink everything that we've just watched - just as we did with Victoria in White Bear.

We suddenly look at Kenny in a completely different light. Before his fight to the death in the woods Kenny tries to commit suicide with the gun the hackers left him for the bank robbery but it turns out it isn't a real gun. The other man clearly looks relieved that his fight will be against the wimpy looking Kenny but - against the odds - Kenny somehow wins the fights and staggers away bloodied and bruised.

As he makes his way home his mother rings and shouts at Kenny because she's heard he was 'looking at kids' online. The hackers - with trollface glee - have released all the dirt they have on everyone. Hector's marriage is over, the woman who was racist is exposed and so on. As for Kenny, a huge police presence is waiting to arrest him - presumably for murder and not merely because of the child porn. Just as in White Bear we are now forced to consider if Kenny really deserves his harsh fate. His life is ruined, his family may disown him and now to cap it all he might get banged up for murder. Shut Up and Dance is clever in the way it invites us to have a tiny degree of compassion for Kenny - despite what he is. It is up to us if we still have sympathy for him - even a more modified and more miniscule sort of sympathy compared to how we felt about him earlier. Shut Up and Dance is a gripping and enjoyably dark episode of Black Mirror with a memorable twist. Best of all this episode feels a lot like the Channel 4 iteration of the show - which is something you can rarely say in season three. This is a great and strangely underrated episode of Black Mirror and one of the high points of season three.

SAN JUNIPERO

(Directed by Owen Harris, Written by Charlie Brooker)

SYNOPSIS - In the party town of San Junipero in 1987, shy young Yorkie (Mackenzie Davis) meekly ventures into a nightclub and is taken with a charismatic girl named Kelly (Gugu Mbatha-Raw). Kelly decides to talk to Yorkie but Yorkie is timid and says she is engaged to be married. The women meet up again later though and go to bed. Yorkie tells Kelly this was her first time. When she later searches for Kelly again, Yorkie seems to be in a different and more modern time period. Kelly tries to shun Yorkie this time and explains that she is dying. It transpires that San Junipero is a virtual reality simulation into which someone's consciousness can be temporarily or permanently downloaded. In reality, Yorkie and Kelly are both elderly women. Yorkie was paralysed at a young age and is now in a coma. She wants to die and live in on San Junipero. Kelly doesn't want to live on in San Junipero when she dies because her daughter passed away before this technology was invented and so her late husband declined to be downloaded into a virtual reality afterlife and preferred to die the 'natural' way to be with his daughter. Kelly's decision means that Yorkie will never see her again and be alone in San Junipero. Will there be a late change of heart from Kelly?

REVIEW - San Junipero is one of the most critically acclaimed episodes of Black Mirror and frequently places in the top three when critics do their episode rankings. You could say this was an uncharacteristic episode at the time as it is optimistic and pleasant and even what you might describe as (in a good way) soppy. Charlie Brooker said that this episode was sort of like a response to those people complaining about Black Mirror becoming too mainstream and American with the move to Netflix. He decided to write a love story with a California type setting just to show that a different type of Black Mirror episode isn't necessarily a bad thing. He plainly succeeded in this goal because San Junipero got a great reception and remains one of the most and famous episodes of Black Mirror.

It was inevitable that the show would sometimes move beyond its grittier and darker roots because you can't make every single episode like The National Anthem or White Bear. The Twilight

Zone, which is the biggest inspiration on Black Mirror, had an eclectic range of episodes from science fiction to horror to more whimsical and comedic fables - even some sentimental stories. Charlie Brooker clearly didn't want to pen himself in too much when it came to the future of the show. He didn't want to have to write another White Christmas each week. He wanted the freedom to do different types of stories if the mood took him. San Junipero is sunny and optimistic and sentimental and works fine as a change of pace. The technology theme is pivotal to this story too - which helps it retain some strong DNA residue.

The Twilight Zone episode which San Junipero, in a roundabout way, evokes the most is Kick the Can. Kick the Can was directed Lamont Johnson and written by George Clayton Johnson. This is a sentimental episode but you'd have to have a heart of stone not to be moved by it. Charles Whitley (Ernest Truex) is a resident of Sunnyvale Rest Home for the elderly. When his son refuses to take him in he becomes depressed but decides that the secret to eternal youth is acting young. He begins to rouse the other residents into having fun but - most of all - he believes a game of "kick the can" will awaken memories of summers long past, freshly cut grass, and lost youth. Something magical might happen but he must persuade them to join him. The most obstinate though is his friend Ben (Russell Collins) who just thinks he's being an old fool. Kick the Can has a great performance by Ernest Truex and a fantastic haunting dreamlike ending with wonderful music by Bernard Herrmann. The coda is the Twilight Zone at its most sublime and magical. This is a moving story about old age, death, youth and friendship with a good supporting cast and an excellent script. San Junipero has a similar theme of elderly people given a way to recapture their lost youth. Kick the Can did this through magic but Black Mirror - appropriately enough - does this through technology.

San Junipero is a little slow to get going initially and feels like a riff on eighties films at first glance - which is hardly original - with the John Hughes fashions and retro arcade machines. This episode doesn't feel much like Black Mirror at all at first but if you stick with it patience is rewarded and the story falls into place in an interesting and fairly satisfying sort of way. The early slowness and vagueness all changes when the twist arrives and we learn that Yorkie and Kelly are in reality two elderly people who are permitted to make limited trips to this virtual reality world where you can be young again and party all night. It's like a virtual fountain of youth. The trips to San Junipero seem to be rationed because you'd probably just want to stay there all the time. If I could be downloaded into San Junipero and wander the beach and go in arcades I'd probably never want to leave. It looks like a wonderful place. There is a big fantasy/reality theme in this episode with San Junipero obviously representing fantasy. We all prefer fantasy to harsh reality but we realise that - sadly - fantasy is not a place you can live full time. But what if it was? San Junipero might be rationed to the living but if you die you could just stay there forever.

Note how San Junipero includes a more edgy downtown area with punk style clubs. It clearly caters to all tastes! The drama in this episode comes from Kelly's reluctance to join Yorkie in San Junipero when her actual body dies. Neither her husband nor daughter used this technology when they passed away so would Kelly somehow be abandoning them if she chose to spend the 'afterlife' in San Junipero with Yorkie rather than place her faith in a spiritual afterlife? On a simple humanist level divorced from religious belief, would she feel guilt if she chose not to die naturally and be laid to rest with her husband and daughter? The concept in this episode certainly provides a lot of food for thought. I suspect that given the option most of us would probably be happy to carry on living in San Junipero after our death - although it isn't perfect. Kelly comments that it can't replicate the tastes and sensations of the real world. One of the strengths of San Junipero is that it has this big and very

Black Mirror technology concept at the heart of the story which is fascinating to ponder on. This is one of the best basic ideas the show has come up with and thankfully the episode is strong enough to do justice to the concept.

Despite the apparent happy ending in this episode too we can't help but ponder on the precarious nature of this San Junipero technological afterlife. The people in San Junipero have basically been downloaded into a tech firm computer programme requiring many servers. But what if the company in charge went bankrupt or simply decided to turn San Junipero off to save money? What if the computer simulation malfunctioned or got hacked? Everyone in San Junipero could just disappear if any of these things happened. What if someone hacked San Junipero and changed it from paradise into a ruined zombie infested nightmare world? San Junipero tugs on the heartstrings when Kelly agrees to marry Yorkie in the real world to sanction her euthanasia and allow them to live together in San Junipero. This is one Black Mirror episode where you don't begrudge a happy ending. Excellent use is made of period songs in this episode like Belinda Carlisle's Heaven Is a Place on Earth and the Smiths' Girlfriend in a Coma. Some might like their Black Mirror to be a trifle darker and twistier but you'd have to a miserable curmudgeon indeed not to be touched by San Junipero. This is a different sort of Black Mirror episode than we are used to but it works fine while still retaining the essential substance and themes of the show.

MEN AGAINST FIRE

(Directed by Jakob Verbruggen, Written by Charlie Brooker)

SYNOPSIS - "Stripe" Koinange (Malachi Kirby) and "Hunter"

Raiman (Madeline Brewer) are soldiers involved in a war against monsters known as 'roaches'. The soldiers have a neural implant called MASS which helps them on their missions. MASS is sort of like a player having skill and weapons upgrades in a video game. MASS gives the soldiers data and an advantage in firefights. Stripe begins to experience glitches in his MASS implant though and these glitches suggest that not all is what it seems when it comes to this war and the true nature of the enemy...

REVIEW - The title Men Against Fire is a reference to S.L.A. Marshall's book about the performance of the US infantry in World War 2. Marshall's research found that a surprisingly large number of soldiers never actually fired their rifle in the war and went out of their way to avoid shooting anyone. The book was basically about ways to improve the infantry as a fighting force but the data about soldiers was interesting because it suggested human empathy and a basic kindness instinct made people reluctant to use force - even in circumstances where it is justified and that is actually your job. Most (though sadly not all) human beings are basically decent and have a safety valve which blocks them from doing bad things to others. They have a conscience and a moral compass. These qualities are not really what you want though if you desire a ruthless fighting machine to fight and exterminate the enemy with no mercy or hesitation. This then is basically the theme of this Black Mirror story. Stripe begins to have empathy for the enemy and see them not (as the propaganda insists) as vermin who need to be exterminated in the name of freedom and survival but as people. Stripe and the soldiers have been conditioned to regard the 'enemy' as evil and a threat to all they know. That turns out to be a long way from the actual truth though. Glitches in Stripe's MASS implant give him a new perspective on the 'war' and the reality of the situation.

The twist of this episode is that the 'roaches' are not monsters at all but an oppressed minority being persecuted and wiped out by a totalitarian system. This obviously makes them analogous to those who suffered under the Nazis but Men Against Fire is essentially a commentary on immigrants and asylum seekers and how they tend to be demonised and scapegoated by politicians on the right of the political spectrum. So you could say then that the message of Men Against Fire is somewhat on the nose. This isn't the most subtle episode when it comes to the themes and messaging. The twist in Men Against Fire - while dramatically sound in the context of the story - is far too predictable for its own good and also not original in the slightest. It mimics the story in a 1985 Outer Limits episode called Hearts and Minds. Hearts and Minds had soldiers manipulated into seeing a human enemy as monsters. Men Against Fire does the same thing in its story. So, if you have watched the Outer Limits revival episode Hearts and Minds then Men against Fire will offer no surprises at all and merely give you a sense of deja vu.

Men Against Fire is arguably the first dud in what has generally been a strong and very watchable season three thus far. This is one of the least interesting episodes of Black Mirror because everything plays out as expected and the tone and story is dull and generic. Men Against Fire just doesn't bring anything new to the Black Mirror table and compared to the Channel 4 years of the show (or even Shut Up and Dance) it feels like bland mainstream anthology fare that you'd get in any number of modern shows. You could imagine this episode slotting into Masters of Horror quite comfortably - which is something you couldn't say about things like The National Anthem or Shut Up and Dance. The problem with Men Against Fire is that you expect something more from Black Mirror than this sort of cookie cutter stuff. One of the other problems with this episode is that near future stories about soldiers fighting a mysterious and shadowy enemy in a vaguely science fiction type of war are not exactly original. You do feel as if you've seen this sort of story all before many times in other things.

Starship Troopers was said to be a big influence on this episode but Men Against Fire is a rather dull experience compared to that fantastic cult film. Men Against Fire does though share the themes of Starship Troopers - where the youthful infantry soldiers are being brainwashed by propaganda and used as cannon fodder to fight an ill defined war for what is clearly an oppressive gung ho fascist regime. The young soldiers in Starship Troopers are actually the villains but are conditioned to believe they are the heroes. Men Against Fire is basically doing the same thing. Stripe and Hunter are villains in this story but are unaware of that - until that is Stripe's implants begin to glitch and the truth is slowly revealed. Now that the real picture is becoming clear, Stripe's humanity has emerged - which is the last thing the regime who sent him into battle want. The twist in Men Against Fire is that the 'roaches' are not monsters (as the MASS system makes them appear) but an oppressed group who are the victims of genocide.

The MASS system is designed to make soldiers lethal and the propaganda ruthless. The 'enemy' is distorted and manipulated into being this evil threat and so the soldiers don't hesitate to shoot. In reality though they are merely exterminating helpless innocent civilians. Once the real situation becomes clear to Stripe it is impossible for him to carry out his orders because he is a human being with feelings. The two leads in episode this are serviceable but this isn't one of those Black Mirror episodes where the acting knocks your socks off. Madeline Brewer, who plays Hunter, would later become best known for playing Janine in The Handmaid's Tale. The standout performance in Men Against Fire comes from Michael Kelly as the slick but sinister psychologist that Stripe has to confide to. While the story of soldiers being manipulated (to commit genocide) is mildly interesting this episode is a little on the slow and derivative side to ever really engage and the big twist falls flat because it is not hard to predict and has already been done in other stories anyway. So in the end Men Against fire becomes something of a chore to get through and never really surprises the viewer. This is a curiously one note episode of Black Mirror which - despite the technology theme - feels generic and obvious.

The military action sequences in the episode don't feel terribly interesting either and run through various tropes like the gung ho hardcase female soldier. You feel like you've seen just about everything in Men Against Fire done better in other shows and films. Stripe eventually rebels against his orders and tries to help the poor people they are supposed to be killing. This lands him in hot water with the awful regime he is fighting for. It transpires that soldiers are told exactly what the MASS system is when they enlist. They are told it manipulates their senses so that they become efficient ruthless killing machines. If they still choose to enlist their memories are wiped so they don't remember being told this. So it turns out that Stripe agreed to all of this when he enlisted - which naturally comes as a shock to him. Stripe is given the choice of having his memory wiped and going back to soldiering with MASS or going to prison. It's a bleak ending - compounded by the last shot of Stripe visiting the house which features in his happy MASS manipulated dreams and finding it derelict and empty. Men Against Fire is competently made but ultimately it's a rather dull and forgettable episode of Black Mirror which isn't helped by having a twist that was already done decades ago by The Outer Limits.

HATED IN THE NATION

(Directed by James Hawes, Written by Charlie Brooker)

SYNOPSIS - Detectives Karin Parke (Kelly Macdonald) and Blue Coulson (Faye Marsay) are assigned to investigate a series of murders in which the victims were people who became online hate figures for their controversial views or actions. It eventually becomes apparent the murders are connected to Autonomous Drone Insects (ADIs) - basically robotic bees designed to help the environment with real bees in decline. The company who make the robotic bees for the government appear to be innocent so it becomes increasingly apparent that the system has been hacked by an outside party. Can the detectives get to the bottom of this strange mystery?

REVIEW - Hated in the Nation tends to divide opinion somewhat and isn't generally considered to be a top tier episode of Black Mirror. This is one of those Black Mirror entries where no one can quite seem to agree whether it is good or mediocre. It does have its fans though. The style and mood is inspired by arty Scandinavian police procedurals and they nail that style pretty well in Hated in the Nation despite the (unavoidably daft at times) science fiction trappings of the story with the deadly robot bee shenanigans.

This is quite a strange episode in that it has this robot been plotline but maintains a serious tone and never leans into the bee antics too heavily. Hated in the Nation is a blend of science fiction horror and police drama and manages to fuse these two disparate elements quite well with no tonal whiplash on behalf of the viewer. This is what you would describe as a solid episode rather than an especially distinguished or memorable one. Hated in the Nation is well made and mildly interesting but it isn't one of those Black Mirror episodes that sticks in the memory or has some bleak twist that everyone talks about.

The biggest problem with this episode is that it runs to almost ninety minutes so is basically a feature length Black Mirror film. To justify a running time of one hour and thirty minutes you need a story which is considerably above average and will fully engage us throughout. I'm not entirely sure that Hated in the Nation is strong enough though to justify such a long running time. The duration does make it drag somewhat in the end and threaten to outstay its welcome but one could argue the extra time does give the story more room to breathe and the characters longer to be developed. All the same though you suspect we wouldn't have missed an awful lot if this story had lost twenty minutes and been presented in a somewhat more compact form. The story in this episode is framed by Detective Chief Inspector Karin Parke speaking at a public inquiry - where she relates this strange and twisty tale of robotic bees and murder. Although this is never the most compelling or exciting Black Mirror episode Hated in the Nation does get a big boost from the strong performances by Kelly Macdonald and Faye Marsay as the leads. These two actors are a solid anchor for the drama that unfolds.

One of the obvious inspirations for this episode was cancel culture and more specifically people getting online hate for things they have said or posted. Charlie Brooker said he experienced this himself when he wrote a column for The Guardian around the time of the 'War on Terror' in which he made a joke alluding to President George W Bush needing to be assassinated. The article was eventually taken offline and Brooker (who later said he probably shouldn't have made the joke in the first place) said he got a lot of violent and threatening messages from people online as a consequence of the joke. Brooker said he found it interesting (and not in a nice way) how easily one can become a hate figure for something you write or say online. The controversial journalist Jo Powers (Elizabeth Berrington) who is found dead at the start of this episode is clearly based on Katie Hopkins. There is seemingly always a gap in the market for a no nonsense right-wing media commentator who rails against (what they perceive to be) political correctness and the way the country is going. Various figures have taken up this grubby baton over the years with varying degrees of infamy and success.

You can guess what these people usually moan about. Too many immigrants, teachers are too woke, the criminal justice system is too soft, Muslims are taking over, we are being taxed too much, there are too many welfare scroungers etc, etc. Katie Hopkins was more insidious in the way that she exploited her reality television fame to appear on all manner of television shows as a commentator on the issue of the day. There was something more troubling about Hopkins than your average conservative rentagob. She was way more offensive than your usual right-leaning Aunt Sally. She started comparing migrants to cockroaches and tweeted about a 'final solution' for Muslims after the tragic bombing of the Ariana Grande concert in Manchester. Hopkins seems to be pretty much beyond the pale these days and is banished from the mainstream. She now seems to exist on the fringes of alternative media. Hated in the Nation was written at a time when Hopkins was more famous than she is today so she was clearly an influence on this story.

Other characters who come under fire in Hated in the Nation include a rapper who makes light of a fan that died and the heartless chancellor Tom Pickering (who is clearly an analogue for the equally heartless George Osborne - the multi-millionaire chancellor who inflicted a merciless austerity drive on Britain's services and working-class people after the 2010 election). The message in Hated in the Nation is not to dispute there are awful people who say stupid offensive things. That much is certain. The broader message of this episode is that online hate and threats of violence should not be a part and parcel of public discourse and the internet. You should be able to disagree with someone and debate them without resorting to threatening to have them killed. Hated in the Nation is not the most original story and evokes a number of things - like the Michael Crichton novel Prey and also No. 6 (which is a Japanese anime). The idea of a 'hit list' of people to be bumped off is not exactly original either but Hated in the Nation does have a nice central conceit in that this technology, designed to do something good, has been hijacked and distorted and become a means for trolls to murder whoever they deem worthy of death. One could say this commentary may reference the internet as a whole. A technology with so much potential for good (like education and communication) but in the hands of the wrong people (chiefly criminals and fraudsters) a tool for a great number of horrible things.

One's enjoyment of Hated in the Nation may in part relate to how much you enjoy police procedurals. It's a little disappointing that Hated in the Nation never goes full on daft killer robot bee caper if truth be told because the bee sequences are quite good fun. There appears to be a plot hole in Hated in the Nation in that the facial recognition software the bees use could presumably be negated by something as simple as wearing a mask but it isn't a huge drawback and only something the more pedantic viewer (like me I suppose!) might mention. The reputation of Hated in the Nation seems to be all over the shop in Black Mirror fandom. Some thought this was an excellent episode while others found it a bit boring to get through (obviously not helped by the unusual length of the story). It's certainly a well made and interesting episode with some tense scenes and good acting but it probably won't be everyone's Black Mirror cup of tea. If you like detective mysteries and a more slow burn sort of narrative you may well enjoy this a lot though. The main problem with Hated in the Nation is that, while quite interesting, it never quite justifies the ninety minute running time and never becomes as intriguing or compelling as you desperately want it to be.

SERIES FOUR (2017)

USS CALLISTER

(Directed by Toby Haynes, Written by William Bridges & Charlie Brooker)

SYNOPSIS - Robert Daly (Jesse Plemons) is a brilliant but

socially awkward programmer who created an amazing multiplayer online game called Infinity which allows one to have a Star Trek type adventure through virtual reality. Daly works at Callister Inc as the chief technology officer. He is embittered though by the fact that the company CEO James Walton (Jimmi Simpson) took his idea for Infinity and made a fortune out of it without affording him the credit and respect he felt he deserved. Daly is further embittered by the fact that the staff at the company don't seem to like to like very much and find him to be creepy. Daly vents his frustration through a secret 'mod' he has created within Infinity. Using stolen DNA from his work colleagues he has trapped clones of them inside the game. Inside the game he is Captain Robert Daly of the USS Callister. The clones, who act as his crew, are mere playthings to him and must be subservient or pay the price...

REVIEW: Black Mirror does Star Trek was the expectation for this episode and USS Callister more or less does exactly that - with a fair sprinkle of Galaxy Quest thrown in for good measure. Toby Haynes, who co-wrote and directed this episode, is a big Star Trek fan so clearly brought a lot of ideas to the table. Oddly, Charlie Brooker has said that he hasn't watched much Star Trek himself so isn't what you would describe as an expert or even fan. This episode is not really a parody or p*** take of Star Trek. It's actually quite affectionate and respectful to its inspiration in places. Star Trek began life as a humble television series in 1966. It was created by Gene Roddenberry who - rather like Rod Serling with The Twilight Zone - had a notion that he could serve up more interesting and topical themes if disguised within the bubble of a science fiction show. Roddenberry had been working as a writer for some time without huge success and was frustrated by the staid and conservative nature of American television at the time.
He came up with a broad outline for Star Trek and pitched it as Wagon Train in Space to pique the curiosity of dubious television networks. The colourful bargain basement series was eventually cancelled after three seasons and the cast went their

separate ways. That seemed to be more or less be the end of it. However, Star Trek unexpectedly became a cult favourite in broadcast syndication and began to slowly mushroom into a cultural phenomenon.

William Shatner said he only realised how popular the defunct show had become when he attended his first Star Trek convention in the seventies and was treated like a pop star. Star Trek offers an attractively optimistic vision of the future where there is no war, disease, poverty or money and the human race has united as one to explore space. Star Trek presents science fiction laced fables about human ethics and moral dilemmas. One of the problems modern Star Trek has sometimes run into is that it forgets this building block and is too focussed on action and space battles. I am a Star Trek fan (primarily the classic series, Next Generation and DS9 - I don't watch the modern Trek shows) myself and enjoyed Galaxy Quest so I got a kick out of USS Callister and enjoyed seeing Black Mirror in this type of playpen. Repeats of The Next Generation are still responsible for me occasionally pretending I've detected a high cluster of graviton particles with the television remote control. Jesse Plemons is able to channel some vintage ham Shatner in this episode as Daly lives out his fantasies in this game - which he based on a series called Space Fleet that he used to watch on television and is clearly an obsessive fan of. The real world is a crushing disappointment to Robert Daly but in the Infinity game he can live out his fantasies and be someone completely different.

Daly seems meek and harmless in the real world but he's a swaggering bully on the USS Callister and not averse to violence and sexual abuse. So you could say there is more of a hint of a subtext about toxic masculinity in this story. Daly, though outwardly placid, is seething with resentment and he uses the Infinity game as a means to vent this frustration and anger at the world. That's bad news for Captain Daly's unfortunate USS Callister crew. The clones of the real Callister

Inc staff suddenly plunged into this game have the memories and personalities of their real life source so are bewildered to be thrust into this situation and suddenly be under the complete control of that creepy Mr Daly from the office. He's unhinged and unpredictable and they must quickly learn to do as he says because he has all the power given this is his own mod. Daly might be a genius but he's also childlike and doesn't really understand people. His immaturity is visually signposted in the episode by the fact he seems to consume nothing but chocolate milk and pizza. Daly is a great and unusual villain in this episode and Jesse Plemons, as ever, is very watchable and interesting in this role.

What is clever about this episode is that it sort of spins away from Daly as the focal point and becomes about the clone of employee Nanette Cole (Cristin Milioti) seeking to rally the Callister crew to mutiny and overthrow the tyrannical rule of Captain Daly. This is easier said than done but Nanette has no intention of being anyone's puppet. So the episode switches to being more of a romp, a sort of heist film with control of the USS Callister the goal. So you get these overlapping tangents to the story. It's all great fun with more comedy than we are generally used to in a Black Mirror story. There are though still plenty of trademark Black Mirror dark moments - like when Captain Daly removes Nanette's facial features so she can't breathe. This is a little homage to a moment in the Joe Dante remake of it's a Good Life in Twilight Zone: The Movie. The original version of It's a Good Life is clearly a major touchstone for USS Callister. The original It's a Good Life was directed by James Shelby and written by Rod Serling from a 1953 short story by Jerome Bixby. In the small town of Peaksville something very strange has happened. The rest of the world has disappeared and Peaksville appears to be alone. Cars, electricity and machines have been taken away and anyone who tries to sing or play a record is in very big trouble indeed.

Everyone in Peaksville must think only pleasant happy thoughts and obey every whim of the terrible controlling monster in their midst. The "monster" and perpetrator of all this misery? An innocent cute looking six year old boy named Anthony Fremont (Bill Mumy). Anthony is no ordinary boy though. He's a conscienceless child with truly terrifying and uncanny psychic abilities. Anthony can make anything he wants happen just by thinking about it. Captain Daly in the mod version of the Infinity game he has created is all powerful. He is Anthony and the USS Callister is his Peaksville. This episode is pretty long at 76 minutes but it flies past and all the Star Trek riffs and references are nicely done. Cristin Milioti (who was later great in that Penguin miniseries) is a charismatic lead and the final fate of Daly (trapped in a shuttlecraft as the game shuts down - his real body comatose in a chair and doomed to die of starvation) is Black Mirror at its bleakest. It's to the credit of the episode that there is never a jarring tonal clash between the comedy and darker elements of the story. Everything blends together into a coherent and satisfying story.

Listen out for Aaron Paul in a small voice part in this episode. You could say that USS Callister is a little Breaking Bad reunion with Plemons and Paul. Paul's condition for appearing in this episode was that it wouldn't preclude him from appearing in a later episode with a bigger role. This of course happened with Beyond the Sea. USS Callister was widely praised and heralded as an instant classic on its release. It would even get a sequel down the line. You'd say that in general this episode lives up to most of the hype. It gives you more or less what you hope for in regard to the 'Black Mirror does Star Trek' premise and is well cast with good spaceship designs and special effects. USS Callister is actually a lot more fun than most of the modern Star Trek output and because this is Black Mirror it also has licence to go very dark when it desires. This gives the episode a nice little edge too to go along with the spangled comedic Star Trek riffs. USS Callister is a very strong and entertaining start to series four. Can the rest of the season live up to this impressive start? Well, let's find out.

ARKANGEL

(Directed by Jodie Foster, Written by Charlie Brooker)

SYNOPSIS - Single mother Marie (Rosemarie DeWitt) is so paranoid after an incident where her child Sara (initially played by a child actor and then Brenna Harding as a teenager) briefly goes missing that she signs up to a high-tech child monitoring system called Arkangel - which is sort of like a way more advanced human version of getting a cat micro-chipped. Marie can now spy on Sara through a tablet and see exactly what she is doing and where her precise location is. The Arkangel system also has a blur filter which prevents Sara from seeing or hearing anything offensive or frightening. But is this control freak parenting going to do Sara more harm than good in the long run? And what will the long term ramifications be for the relationship between mother and daughter?

REVIEW - This episode was directed by Jodie Foster - who also had some creative input into the story and made a few changes. It's a slightly atypical Black Mirror episode because it has a blue collar backdrop and is for the most part more of a slow burn mother/daughter drama than something full of shocks and twists and wild science fiction trappings. The fact that mother and daughter are eventually going to have a big falling out in this story is rather predictable if truth be told and Arkangel never really subverts our expectations in any major way. It more or less goes exactly where you presume it will go - which is slightly disappointing. The surface message of this tale is who would be a parent? You can't win whatever you do. Arkangel obviously also explores the themes of constrictive over protective parenting and the right to privacy when it comes to surveillance type technology. It's fine for Marie to snoop on Sara for safety reasons through Arkangel when Sara is a tiny little girl but this snooping becomes more problematic when Sara hits her mid teens and Marie resorts to the Arkangel technology again. While it is good to be able to locate your child whenever you desire for safety reasons you'd probably be better off not knowing about every single thing that your teenage child might be doing or saying in private.

Marie pulls the tablet out for the first time in years when Sara is no longer a little girl and now in her mid-teens. Marie wants to know if Sara has lied about what she is doing and where she is going that night. Sure enough, it turns out that Sara was economical with the truth. Marie is mortified when the Arkangel technology reveals that Sara (who is now fifteen) is having sex and snorting coke with her boyfriend Trick (Owen Teague). Marie, without telling Sara, warns Tick to stay away from her daughter and then slips the unwitting Sara an abortion medication. So the basic story has Marie still trying to control every aspect of her daughter's life - even when her daughter is no longer a little kid and nearing her late teens. This is all the last straw for Sara and she ends up beating her mother to a pulp with the Arkangel tablet that was used to spy on her. The thing is though the Arkangel filter (which prevents Sara from seeing anything unpleasant) means she can't see how badly she is hurting her mother - which is what you might call darkly ironic! Arkangel is sort of interesting at times but never that compelling or surprising. This is one of those Black Mirror episodes where you are never entirely convinced that the story was interesting or entertaining enough to be turned into an episode in the first place.

Arkangel tends to be ranked as one of the more middling and forgettable episodes of Black Mirror and you can see why. There is little in this episode that stands out or lodges in the memory. It's a competent drama with a technology theme but not an especially memorable or accomplished Black Mirror story. The acting in Arkangel is fine (if nothing to write home about) and the detached and aloof atmosphere generated by the direction is very Black Mirror. The story though is never really that interesting and quite predictable in the end. We learn that the Arkangel technology is banned in Europe and soon to be banned in the United States. Years later though Marie is able to reactivate it using an old tablet - which doesn't have perfect logic. I suppose one must just suspend disbelief and not ask too many questions in this story. The most interesting section of the film is when the young Sara has the world filtered through Arkangel so she doesn't see anything which might alarm her (like a barking dog). We see the older Sara (sans Arkangel) at school shown all manner of gross things on the internet - which must have been an eye-opener for someone so sheltered as a kid. But the story never really leans in this too much besides having Sara self-harm because she's never seen blood before. That probably would have made a more interesting story. How does someone who was shielded from the world cope when that censored world is then revealed to them in all of its imperfect and frightening glory?

Marie's 'helicopter parenting' is sort of understandable because she only has one child but it doesn't do Sara any good in the long run. The ethics of the surveillance become more questionable when Marie resorts to the tablet again when Sara is in her mid-teens. You can understand though why Marie would be aghast that her fifteen year-old daughter is snorting coke and having sex. Arkangel walks a tightrope in terms of character perceptions and although Marie is the villain of the piece we do feel a pang of sympathy for her when Sara walks away at the end. Marie has lost the thing most precious to her but it was all her own fault. She was too possessive and intrusive. It all became too weird and constrictive for Sara in the end. She had to break free from the control of her mother - and Arkangel - to taste genuine freedom and privacy. The moral of this story seems to be that you can't shield children from the world forever. They have to learn from experience.

Marie has been blind all along because by watching her daughter through the prism of the tablet and wrapping her up in this filtered censored version of reality she has not only harmed her child's development and independence but also neglected to provide first hand traditional parenting. Marie can't cope when Sara finally goes out into the world without Arkangel. She basically wants her daughter on that tablet screen forever.

Arkangel is a solid episode that is well directed and has some interesting ideas but ultimately it isn't tremendously entertaining or surprising. It's watchable but never much more than that and with Black Mirror you tend to expect a bit more than something which is merely watchable with plot developments you can see coming a mile off. As a drama about a mother/daughter relationship and constrictive parenting, Arkangel is generally ok but as an episode of Black Mirror it leaves something to be desired. One can't hekp feeling that the potential of the core premise was somewhat squandered here in the end. The story of someone being only able to view a censored and sanitised version of the world but then at some point having to experience life without those high-tech blinkers has a lot of potential and could have been compelling but Arkangel never really goes in on this aspect of the story and seems more interested in being a study of an overbearing and over protective mother. The one saving grace with this episode is that it clocks in at under an hour so isn't the longest Black Mirror story by any stretch. If this had been one of those extra long Black Mirror stories I suspect that Arkangel might well have become a slog to get through in the end.

CROCODILE

(Directed by John Hillcoat, Written by Charlie Brooker)

SYNOPSIS - Rob (Andrew Gower) and Mia Nolan (Andrea

Riseborough) are driving home on a rural lakeside road after a party. Both are drunk and the car is on a quiet road with no people around for miles - all except for one unlucky person. Rob hits and kills a cyclist but rather than report the incident they throw the body into a lake and flee. Fifteen years later Mia is now a celebrated architect with a young son. She hasn't seen Rob for many years. Rob turns up out of the blue and says he believes they should tell the widow of the cyclist what happened through an anonymous note so she can finally get some closure and move on. Mia is against this idea because she fears the note might somehow be traced back to them and put everything she has achieved at risk. She kills Rob during an argument and disposes of the body. It transpires though that there was an incident where a person was run over by a self-driving truck outside the hotel where Mia and Rob argued and a dentist is a potential witness because he saw Mia in the window. An insurance investigator named Shazia (Kiran Sonia Sawar) is assigned to investigate the self-driving truck incident and uses a technology called 'Recaller' where people's memories can be accessed and viewed. Shazia eventually discovers that Mia was a potential witness to the self-driving truck accident but having her memories accessed is going to expose the two deaths Mia was involved in. How far will Mia now go to protect her secrets?

REVIEW - Crocodile is what you might describe as another 'Nordic Noir' inspired Black Mirror. It was shot in Iceland and has some beautifully bleak ice glazed backdrops. The technology that Shazia uses to view memories is intrusive and a clear violation of privacy but it is apparently against the law to refuse to comply if you are asked by an insurance investigator or the authorities to submit to this technology for a case. The technology - though open to abuse in the wrong hands - is clearly something which has positives too because it's a fairly fool proof way of solving crimes or getting to the bottom of accidents. The Recaller technology would certainly make crime cases and court trials a lot easier. Shazia isn't interested in snooping on people and seeing what they've been up to in their private lives. She merely wants to complete her work on the self-driving truck accident so she can paid and move onto another case. Unknown to Sharia though she is treading on dangerous ground by investigating the increasingly ruthless and unhinged Mia. This is one of those Black Mirror stories where a character is haunted by the past. Mia is desperate to to close off her past but this proves a lot more complex than she bargained for. The past is slowly but surely hunting her down and this makes her actions increasingly extreme. The Recaller technology is Mia's worst nightmare because if used on her it shall reveal she was personally involved in two deaths and didn't report either of them to the police.

Crocodile tends not to be regarded as a classic episode of Black Mirror but I quite like this one because at its core, once you strip everything away, it is basically Black Mirror doing a serial killer drama. Mia is so desperate to protect and preserve the nice life and status she has accrued she is perfectly willing to murder anyone who might threaten that. So this episode sort of becomes a very black comedy (not that it was probably intended to be) where you have this female architect embarking on a murder spree to prevent her dark secrets coming to the fore and ruining the nice life she has built for herself. Literally no one is safe if they threaten to uncover Mia's past and put her future at risk. Shazia eventually visits Mia to use the Recaller technology because Mia was a witness to the self-driving hit accident. Mia is well aware this is going to be curtains for her and the deaths of the cyclist and Rob will land her in prison most likely for a very long time. So she decides she has no option but to murder Shazia. She also uses the Recaller technology on Shazia and learns that Shazia's husband knew she was going to Mia's house. So Mia now goes to the house and murders Shazia's husband. It doesn't stop there. Shazia has a baby son and Mia murders him too. She is determined to leave no links at all.

Crocodile has some of that bleak early Black Mirror DNA and the mood and style of this episode is not entirely dissimilar to something like The Entire History of You. However, there is something missing here compared to this show at its very best and so Crocodile never threatens to crack the Black Mirror top table. It's a solid enough effort though and one of those Black Mirror entries that tends to be somewhat underrated. Crocodile's plot doesn't really stand up to very close scrutiny if you think about it too much. Wouldn't Shazia's employers know that she was visiting Mia and was then never seen again? This would make Mia the first person they'd want to talk to. Shazia presumably left notes and electronic files indicating Mia was someone she was about to visit. You'd think then that Mia would eventually get a visit from the authorities asking about Shazia and then be subjected to the Recaller technology again. They wouldn't need to be Columbo to work out that Mia was someone they needed to interview. At the end Mia appears to have got away with it. She's watching her son in a school performance of Bugsy Malone (Jodie Foster Easter egg) and seems happy. But the police arrive and move in.

It transpires that Shazia's son was blind so the Recaller technology could not not have been used on him to determine the killer. A cruel Twilight Zone style twist because Mia didn't need to kill the child. But then comes the (more risible) kicker. The baby had a pet guinea pig who was in the room. The Recaller technology is used on the guinea pig and exposes Mia as the killer. It's a rather daft final twist that probably won't please everyone. This script was originally designed for a male lead but Andrea Riseborough, who was initially up for the part of the insurance investigator, lobbied for the lead role - which then obviously underwent a gender change. While some felt that it was unrealistic that Mia would be physically capable of murdering people and moving bodies it isn't a tremendous leap of imagination because female serial killers do actually exist (Juana Barraza, Irina Gaidamachuk, Piroska Jancsó Ladányi, Lizzie Halliday, Clementine Barnabet, Dorothea Puente, Aileen

Wuornos etc, etc). The gender flip of the main character makes Crocodile more interesting (one might argue this episode would have come off as a bleak riff on Dexter with a male lead) and it worked to the advantage of the episode because it gives us a terrific lead performance by Andrea Riseborough.

Crocodile is not the most memorable episode of Black Mirror and very slow burn but it has captivating locations and good performances. The grisly desperation of Mia to stop her past from ruining her present gives the story plenty of drama and weight. Crocodile is generally what you would describe as a solid if unspectacular episode of Black Mirror. The double twist at the end is probably over-egging the pudding somewhat too. On the whole though this is an interesting serial killer drama that keeps one largely engaged and works well enough for what it is. The last twist does feel a trifle too much though - as if they felt they needed something extra at the end to make the episode more memorable. The use of the technology theme in this episode is quite interesting and helps the story. We see that Mia is trying to block out the Recaller tech and distract it with other memories. it's a bit like being hypnotised but resisting the hypnosis. in the end though Mia's efforts prove fruitless. Some memories are too strong to be blocked out or evaded when subject to this technology. I don't think many people would argue the case for Crocodile being one of the very best episodes of Black Mirror but it is perfectly competent and watchable as far as the more middle-ranking episodes of the show go.

HANG THE DJ

(Directed by Tim Van Patten, Written by Charlie Brooker)

SYNOPSIS - Frank (Joe Cole) and Amy (Georgina Campbell) use dating technology called 'Coach' which matches them up with different partners but for limited (and varying) amounts of time. The couples meet in a luxury rural retreat which is sort of like a more modern version of the village from The Prisoner. Frank and Amy get on exceptionally well during their time together but do not become intimate - which they regret when the time is up and they are parted to be matched with new partners. When they are matched up again they are only given an hour together so Amy decides they should run away from this retreat and ecape together...

REVIEW - This episode has a lot of similarities to San Junipero in that it is a love story with the same sort of twist and also a happy and optimistic ending. So this is one of the 'nice' episodes of Black Mirror and doesn't have the bleakness which is more or less the trademark of the show. Hang the DJ (the title is obviously taken from the song Panic by The Smiths) is generally well regarded and a likeable sort of episode which offers a respite from all the darkness and misery we typically enjoy in Black Mirror! You'd probably say this episode isn't as memorable or atmospheric as San Junipero but it works fine on its own terms. The crucial factor in why this episode works is the believable chemistry between Joe Cole and Georgina Campbell as the two leads. How many times do you watch a film or television show where the romantic leads have no romantic chemistry (or any chemistry at all) and thus fail to sell the central plank of the story? That definitely isn't the case in Hang the DJ because Cole and Campbell have terrific romantic and comedic chemistry and make you completely buy the idea that these two characters are soulmates destined to be together. Whoever cast this episode certainly deserves their money and Hang the DJ enjoys a big boost from the natural chemistry between the two leads.

This story has some vague similarities with the film The Lobster in that these people are all herded together and required to pair off as if being single is the worst thing in the world and like having leprosy or something. It's all voluntary of course though. These people are desperate to find their dream romantic partner and so willing to put themselves through various matchmaking experiments in that elusive quest for Mr or Mrs Right. The story in Hang the DJ is inspired by modern dating sites and also Spotify. Charlie Brooker came up with the idea of these characters having to compile a sort of dating playlist before a final selection is made. The situation the characters find themselves in doesn't look very appealing but that's maybe the point because this is all a simulation to test compatibility. There are some nice moments of deadpan comedy when Frank and Amy are separated and forced to spend time with partners they have no great rapport with. There is nothing worse than being manacled to someone you have nothing in common with and don't even like very much and Hang the DJ manages to glean some good comic moments from this sort of scenario. In order to find the right person Frank and Amy are also required to experience the wrong person.

This episode was shot at Painshill (a park and gardens in Surrey) and looks terrific. I gather that Charlie Brooker was initially uncertain over whether or not to have a happy ending in this story like San Junipero because he feared that fans might think Black Mirror was becoming too soft and soppy. In the end though he did go for an optimistic ending and the largely positive reception to this episode indicates this was the right approach - although some might possibly find Hang the DJ a trifle sentimental for their tastes. One criticism of this episode, and it's a relatively minor complaint in the grand scheme of things, is that the algorithmic matchmaking plot is a simplification of human relationships and comes off as rather clinical. One could argue though that the concept is the natural chemistry and compatibility of Frank and Amy transcending the dating algorithms. The twist in this episode is that this is all a computer simulation - so it is basically a lot like the twist in San Junipero. The Coach technology runs 1000 simulations to see if two people match and in the simulation Frank and Amy rebelled against the rules and tried to run away together 998 times out of 1000. This obviously means they are a match because they are willing to break the rules to be together. The simulations have proved beyond all doubt that these two people will get on like a house on fire.

Their escape attempt is a Truman Show style scene where they hit the border of reality. Hang the DJ reminds me somewhat of the Night Gallery segment Midnight Never Ends where the characters discover they are not real and purely fictional. The end cuts to the real Frank and Amy in a pub. They look across at each other. The dating app has declared them a 99% match due to the simulations. It's a sweet ending - although not exactly impossible to predict. Little clues that Frank and Amy might not be in a real place are scattered throughout the episode. Hang the DJ is far from perfect. Though well acted and generally satisfying as a piece of drama Hang the DJ can never quite escape the fact that an episode about dating and matchmaking is not exactly the most thrilling or compelling of Black Mirror experiences. Hang the DJ is a very pleasant episode though and serves as a nice palette cleanser among the darker episodes in series four. At 50 minutes it doesn't outstay its welcome and the trump card is plainly the chemistry of the two leads - which just goes to show you the importance of casting because if the actors playing Frank and Amy had no chemistry Hang the DJ would not have worked nearly as well as it does. Hang the DJ may well have sunk with bland casting.

You wouldn't say this episode was as successful as San Junipero but it's good for what it is if perhaps a trifle overrated in the Black Mirror gallery as a whole. This is another of those episodes which feels a bit lightweight for Black Mirror but as a riff on dating apps and the pressure society sometimes puts on people to pair up it works fairly well. The twist is not exactly original though because we've seen similar twists in Black Mirror let alone other anthology shows. While the bleakness of Black Mirror is part of its appeal Hang the DJ is resolute in its determination to veer away from this expectation and give you a nice ending. On those terms the ending works fine and because we are invested in the lead characters we have no complaints. Hang the DJ does what it sets out to do and is generally a very good episode but it isn't the type of Black Mirror story you want too many of because there are only so many times you can try and riff on San Junipero and hope to get similar impact.

METALHEAD

(Directed by Tim Van Patten, Written by Charlie Brooker)

SYNOPSIS - In a grim post apocalyptic landscape almost completely devoid of people, Bella (Maxine Peake) and her companions scavenge a warehouse. However, they unwittingly awaken a deadly robotic dog which is designed to hunt and kill humans. Bella is the only survivor of this encounter but is now in big trouble because the robotic dog is on her trail and almost impossible to fight or shake off...

REVIEW: This episode was directed by David Slade - who directed the films Hard Candy and 30 Days of Night. It's a short episode (41 minutes) and probably the least plot driven Black Mirror of all. There is no story to speak of and no satire or allegory. One could though I suppose venture a connection between the robot dog in Metalhead and modern drone warfare. In both cases a lethal technology can dish out death and misery and be used for surveillance without any human being (besides the poor blighter on the receiving end) having to be placed in danger. This episode is just a deadly fight for survival between Bella and a robot dog that is armed to the teeth and programmed to kill. So you get quite an enjoyable sense of whiplash if you come straight into this from Hang the DJ. You go from a bunch of well heeled people at a country retreat to a bleak yarn about a woman being hunted down by a robot. That's the whole point of an anthology show. We never quite know what we are going to get next. Metalhead is shot in black and white to add to the bleak atmosphere. This doesn't come across as a gimmick or pretentious. It genuinely helps the atmosphere. This is a world where darkness and desperation now rules the roost. If you thought Black Mirror was getting too soppy on occasion with the move to Netflix then Metalhead should be up your alley because this story has bleakness to spare.

While this episode was not everyone's cup of tea (it seems to have a fairly low reputation among Black Mirror fandom) its simplicity and leanness actually makes for a nice change of pace. If you do an anthology show it would seem strange not to try something new now and again and Metalhead is definitely what you could describe as experimental. One could argue too that Metalhead is very in keeping with the underlying themes of Black Mirror because it depicts a dystopian future where technology is quite literally out to kill you. Metalhead obviously owes a lot to the 1984 film The Terminator and the dogged pursuit of Bella by the robotic dog evokes the plight of Dennis Weaver in Spielberg's Duel and Richard Benjamin in Westworld. Both are hunted by an unstoppable force - a huge truck and Yul Brynner's gunslinger android respectively. The robot dog is every bit as tenacious and dangerous as the truck and robot cowboy. You definitely wouldn't want this relentless artificial dog after you. Metalhead is also somewhat reminiscent of the mildly cultish Richard Stanley film Hardware. Hardware is a science fiction horror film set in a post-apocalyptic future and stars Dylan McDermott. It follows a young man who moves into a new apartment and discovers a mysterious robotic armour that comes to life and begins to wreak havoc.

The robot dog in Metalhead feels very inspired by the robot dog called Toby in Alan Moore's brilliant comic The Ballad of

Halo Jones. The dog in Metalhead was also influenced by BigDog - a robot designed by Boston Dynamics. So you got a range of influences in Metalhead - which might partly explain why this episode doesn't seem to be terribly well regarded. For some critics and viewers this episode came off as derivative (riffing on old science fiction and horror sources as it does) and lacked the clever plot and twists of the more lauded Black Mirror episodes. You get no explanation for anything in Metalhead. You don't learn why the world is like this or who created the robotic dogs out to kill everyone. You are simply plunged into this nightmarish scenario but that's fine. It's nice to just get a no frills episode like this where the premise is basic and simply boils down to whether Bella can survive or not. The minimalist approach to Metalhead with little in the way of story or dialogue works well if one is partial to this type of lo-fi horror yarn. This episode is basically one long chase and battle to the death and the antagonist is formidable enough to make us feel genuine peril and danger for Bella. On the terms then of a completely stripped down back to basics episode Metalhead is quite unlike anything Black Mirror has done before. The bleak atmosphere is also a strength and gives Metalhead a sombre and edgy sort of feel.

The central theme of Metalhead could be that technology has proved to be the downfall of humanity. Whether this is by design or accident though we aren't quite sure. The end reveals that a box in the warehouse is full of teddy bears. This represents humanity and goodness in a bleak and unforgiving world. One of those toys would mean a lot to a child but securing one unwittingly unleashes a lethal killing machine. This episode is a bit like being inside an immersive survival horror game. We definitely wouldn't want to be in the shoes of the central protagonist. Metalhead feels a lot like a low-budget independent science fiction horror film stretched out to a longer format and on those terms is very watchable and quite gripping. Here perhaps lies one of the problems that some had with Metalhead. Is this really a ten minute short film with the simple premise stretched out well beyond its means at 40 minutes? The bleak atmosphere in Metalhead is heightened by our nagging suspicion that Bella is in over her head and fighting a battle she can't win. Even when she does get the better of the robot dog she is left with shrapnel embedded in her which will allow the other robotic dogs to track her. Some of the shrapnel is impossible to remove without killing herself.

So there is at times a hopeless and futile quality to Bella's duel with the robot dog which feels very Black Mirror. As much as anything Metalhead is about the instinct for survival. Despite the desperate situation Bella never gives up and gamely fights the dog to a standstill. At the end we see her saying goodbye on her walkie-talkie so she clearly has loved ones somewhere. The performance by Maxine Peake in this episode is excellent and continues the great casting in season four. The robot dog is an impressive creation and creepy in the way that it mimics the movements of a real dog. It even wails and the dog rests to recharge when it has Bella trapped up a tree. The fact that Metalhead is an atypical sort of Black Mirror episode works to its advantage. This is an anthology show so you have licence to do different sorts of episodes and try new things. Apparently the original concept for this episode was to have no dialogue at - which would have been interesting. Charlie Brooker said that in his early draft of the script there was going to be a human controller 'piloting' the robotic dog from his home. You would see the controller take a break now and again to tend to his kids. This would have added a cruel and mundane counterpoint to the horror experienced by Bella but in the end they discarded this stuff.

You can attempt to fill in some of the blanks in the story for yourself in Metalhead. Bella takes refuge in a mansion but the robot dogs seem to know this place well. It could be the case that the dogs were once controlled but the inventors lost control over their creation. Or maybe the dogs were used by the powers that be in a genocide or to quash an uprising. Who knows?

Metalhead tends not to be thought of as a vintage episode of Black Mirror but this is grim gripping stuff if you have a sweet tooth for this type of horror. Metalhead has a very middling IMDB score but I don't quite understand that because this is a taut and compelling horror episode which does exactly what it promises on the tin. As we mentioned, I think a possible weakness for some with Metalhead is that it feels rather like a weird short film which has been padded out into a longer format. For some critics this episode just didn't amount to much and lacked originality. One could actually argue though that Metalhead is rather underrated when it comes to Black Mirror episodes and serves as an interesting departure for season four.

BLACK MUSEUM

(Directed by Colm McCarthy, Written by Charlie Brooker)

SYNOPSIS - Nish (Letitia Wright) is a British woman who visits a remote desert museum curated by Rolo Haynes (Douglas Hodge), a disgraced scientist/inventor and collector of technological artefacts. As Nish explores the exhibits, Rolo recounts the dark stories behind each item...

REVIEW - Black Museum is an episode that seems to be held in higher esteem by fans than critics. Some of the critic reviews for this episode were snooty and dismissive but it has an excellent IMDB score so the general public obviously disagreed with the critics on this one. I'm with the fans rather than the critics when it comes to Black Museum because this episode is a lot of fun in that characteristically bleak Black Mirror fashion. Black Museum is structured like an anthology horror film with three different stories all framed by the storyteller Rolo in the museum with Nish. Black Museum obviously has a lot in common with White Christmas in the way it is structured around three tales told through a framing device or wraparound. This episode is not as strong as White Christmas but it's pretty good for what it is. The museum is liberally scattered with little references to previous Black Mirror episodes which are fun for fans to spot. The title of this episode takes its name from the crime museum of London's Metropolitan Police Service - where artifacts from notorious killers and crime figures are displayed. It's now called the Crime Museum but it used to be called the Black Museum. John Haigh's gloves and apron (which he used to protect himself from burns from the acid bath he disposed of victims with) are displayed at New Scotland Yard's infamous museum. The museum has also displayed Dennis Nilsen's cooking stove. Nilsen sometimes used this stove to boil the heads of his victims. Anyway, the framing device of Rollo and Nish in the museum is very good.

An influence on this episode was Tales from the Crypt. Tales from the Crypt was a cult horror anthology television series based on the infamous and influential (everyone from Stephen King to George Romero grew up loving them) 1950s EC horror and suspense comics published by William Gaines. The enjoyably lurid and colourful comics (which were rather gruesome and risqué, although tongue-in-cheek and with their own twisted sense of morality) offered all manner of deaths, monsters, zombies, murders, ghosts, and general macabre mayhem stirred by greed, lust and envy until parents began to notice what their children were reading and the comics were banned, even becoming the subject of Congressional subcommittee hearings. The television series became something of a phenomenon after its debut in 1989 and ran for seven seasons until 1996. Why did it work so well? The show had very solid foundations right from the start with Richard Donner, David Giler, Walter Hill, Joel Silver and Robert Zemeckis as executive producers and was consequently able to attract some notable directors and actors. It was also a HBO cable show and so didn't have to worry about censorship.

Another possible influence on Black Museum is Tales from the Hood. Tales from the Hood is an underrated anthology directed by Rusty Cundieff. This was produced by Spike Lee and gives you four stories of urban horror that touch on themes like racism and gang culture. The first tale in Black Museum concerns Dr Peter Dawson (Daniel Lapaine). Dawson created an implant which allowed him to feel exactly what a patient is feeling - thus helping him diagnose what the patient is suffering from and coming up with the appropriate treatment. However, Dawson became addicted to the sensations of pain and this turned him murderous and insane. This yarn was based on a story by the magician Penn Jillette. i gather that Penn Jillette wanted to play Rolo in this episode but the production and casting was too far down the line for this to be possible. While I'm sure he would have been good we didn't miss too much because Douglas Hodge is excellent in Black Museum. This first story has a nasty edge - which is fun in a Re-Animator sort of way. One of the enjoyable things about Black Museum is that it fully embraces its mission statement to be a horror episode and goes all in on the horror anthology format.

In the next story Rolo tells Nish how he persuaded Jack (Aldis Hodge) to transfer his comatose wife Carrie's (Alexandra Roach) consciousness into Jack's brain so that she could experience life again and he could have some contact with her. As a result of this they shared the same body - which obviously led to all manner of complications and became increasingly untenable. For example, what was Jack supposed to do if he dated a woman? That could be rather awkward couldn't it? So in the end Jack was given a function to pause Carrie and she was only allowed to inhabit his brain at weekends. Jack's new girlfriend wanted Carrie deleted though so Carrie ended up being transferred into a stuffed monkey toy. Suffice to say the stories in this anthology are not a barrel of laughs and rather bleak - which may explain why fans tend to like this episode more than the critics did. With a few adjustments you could imagine Black Museum slotting into the Channel 4 years of the show. Being trapped in a stuffed monkey toy is not much fun for Carrie because the monkey can only say two phrases. Rolo tells Nish that the technology used to transfer Carrie was later banned. You could say that Rolo serves the function of mad scientist in this episode. He's like Dr Herbert West - only a man of technology rather than science and medicine.

The final yarn concerns Clayton Leigh (Babs Olusanmokun). Leigh was convicted of murder and on death row permitted Rolo to create a hologram of him that visitors could put in the electric chair and execute - with the hologram experiencing actual pain. Though you might think this a strange thing to do there were apparently plenty of sadists and sickos out there delighted to have their own hologram to torture and execute. It transpires that Nish is really Leigh's daughter. She's actually American and was putting on a fake British accent to disarm Rolo. She has poisoned Rolo with some water he accepted from her (Nish secretly disabled the air conditioning to make him feel hot and thirsty). Nish sets fire to the museum and leaves with the hologram of her father and the stuffed monkey toy with Carrie's consciousness. The episode suggests that Nish might be planning to transfer Carrie from the monkey to San Junipero - which would be a nice gesture. Nish rescuing her hologram father is less of a sweet coda though because the museum offered guests souvenirs of Leigh to electrocute at home whenever they felt like it! So even the ending of Black Museum is what you might describe as bittersweet. There are still plenty of holograms of Leigh out there being tortured and electrocuted.

If you have a sweet tooth for anthology horror films then Black Museum is a lot of fun and definitely didn't deserve some of the sniffy reviews it got from critics. The thing people tend to like anthology horror films is that if one particular story doesn't float your boat then there'll be a completely different one along soon so you don't have to worry. Black Museum, on a smaller scale, works like that but none of the individual stories are clunkers or a slog to get through. Letitia Wright and Douglas Hodge are also very good in the framing scenes and help anchor the episode and the way the wraparound becomes part of the story and tied into the segments is nicely done. Black Museum is an enjoyable way to end what has been an interesting and solid season of Black Mirror. While Arkangel didn't set the world alight and not everyone like Metalhead, season five had no out and out clunkers and offered a fairly consistent run of episodes. You'd probably say season four is stronger overall than season three and it is vastly superior to the upcoming season five. Black Museum is a fun horror episode on the whole. it's a bit daft in places and probably stand up to close scrutiny but it is strange, bleak and the technology theme is to fore. I'm always happy to get a horror anthology type episode in Black Mirror and while Black Museum is no White Christmas it is perfectly watchable and entertaining in its own right.

INTERACTIVE FILM (2018)

BANDERSNATCH

(Directed by David Slade, Written by Charlie Brooker)

SYNOPSIS - It is 1984. The computer game market in Britain is big business with many kids (and adults) buying games for their Spectrum or Commodore 64. Stefan Butler (Fionn Whitehead) is adapting a book into a 'Choose Your Own Adventure' computer game where you have to make choices which then affect what happens next in the game. Stefan pitches the game to Tuckersoft - which is run by Mohan Thakur (Asim Chaudhry) and has genius star programmer Colin Ritman (Will Poulter) on its staff. Stefan is given the option of working with Tuckersoft to finish the game or complete it on his own at home. But it is us, the viewer, who decides what decisions Stefan makes in Bandersnatch because this episode of Black Mirror is an interactive 'Choose Your Own Adventure' story. As he struggles to complete his game Stefan becomes paranoid and troubled and convinced that he is being manipulated by some outside force beyond his control...

REVIEW - 'Choose Your Own Adventure' style books for kids were quite a big thing in the past. I can distinctly remember owning a 'Find Your Fate' Indiana Jones book as a child where you were given two options and then had to turn to the corresponding page to see how your decision panned out. Sometimes the page just simply told you that the wrong decision was made and you were now dead or something. So while these sorts of books were fun for a time they could get frustrating and have one yearning for a more traditional narrative in the end. And this, I think, is part of the problem with Bandersnatch and why it didn't quite hit the bullseye for some viewers. You could probably call this episode an interesting and ambitious experiment which doesn't quite come off in the end. It doesn't quite work as well as you want it to. The term "bandersnatch" originates from a fictional creature created by Lewis Carroll. The more salient reference here though is a game Imagine Software were working on in real life in 1984. They planned to release two 'mega' games which would offer a huge technological advance on the competition. One of these games was titled Bandersnatch but it never came out because Imagine Software went bust in 1984. I'd recommend watching the BBC 2 documentary (Commercial Breaks) which was shot in 1984 and covered the collapse of Imagine. This documentary is a fascinating insight into the business of computer games in 1984 and was clearly an influence on the office designs and Tuckersoft in Bandersnatch.

There is a meta element to this episode (beyond the interactive approach) in that you sort of have the illusion of free will but in actuality probably don't - which echoes the plight of Stefan in the story. Bandersnatch, as a concept (if not a story), rather evokes Dragon's Lair. Dragon's Lair is a laserdisc video game published by Cinematronics in 1983. The game was unique because it featured animation by ex-Disney animator Don Bluth. It was a lavish and enticing looking game and had the player taking the role of Dirk the Daring, a knight attempting to rescue Princess Daphne from the evil dragon Singe. However, the game was not a game in the sense that other arcade games were games. In Dragon's Lair you made a series of choices and then watched what happened to Dirk next as a consequence of your choice. It was sort of like a 'choose your fate' adventure rather than the joystick waggling, button pressing action romp gamers were used to playing. Because of this, Dragon's Lair was a frustrating, not to mention expensive experience. You either got fed up watching Dirk die or learned the pattern to beat the game. Either option cost you a lot of money. Dragon's Lair didn't have the long lasting appeal that Bluth might have hoped (although it was ported to numerous home gaming systems with varying degrees of success) and wasn't the industry game changer it seemed to be at the time but - for a brief moment - Dragon's Lair was all the rage and the main attraction of arcades in the early eighties. The game Stefan is making is sort of like Dragon's Lair sans the fancy cartoon animation.

Obvious influences on Bandersnatch include Donnie Darko and Ubik by Philip K. Dick - which is about a surreal, shifting universe where the boundaries between life and death blur. There are plainly allusions to Alice in Wonderland and we see characters sampling LSD - the latter chiming with Colin Ritman's fondness for conspiracy theories. Most conspiracy theories tend to develop cracks if subjected to scrutiny and some just fall apart altogether if one looks too closely. That can't be said of Project MKUltra - something which sounds EXACTLY like a conspiracy theory but is actually true. From 1953 to 1973, the CIA funded experiments in order to learn how to control people for the purposes of spying. These experiments were designed to see if the human mind could be altered or controlled. The psychedelic drug LSD was a big part of the experiments and sensory deprivation chambers were used. The origins of the project are thought to have come from a fear that the Soviet Union was much more advanced in brainwashing techniques. This was a sphere of the Cold War that America was apparently losing and so was born (after several similar if smaller projects) MKUltra. For the CIA, the worst-case scenario was that the Soviet Union could find a way mind control US military and intelligence officials. It all sounds somewhat crazy but experiments in psychological techniques were very real. The project only became public in 1975 after a congressional investigation into CIA activities.

There are some nice period details in Bandersnatch - not just the soundtrack of 80s hits. Colin finds Stefan's taste in music (The Thompson Twins indeed) dreadful so makes him a playlist. The character of Colin riffs on the 'whizz kid' stories about software houses at the time. There were some newspaper stories about how some genius schoolkid had been signed up to make computer games and now drove around in a Ferrari or something. While a lot of these stories were exaggerated and embellished for publicity it is true that software houses hired some very young people to make games for them. The computer game offices in this episode feel authentic and realistic and Bandersnatch nicely captures a sense of time and place. Companies like Tuckersoft would potentially have made a lot of money in 1984 - but only if they could deliver good games on time. This was one of the drawbacks of that era of gaming. Companies, rushed for time and faced with impossible deadlines, would sometimes release shoddy games beset with bugs. It was easier to get away with that in those days because there was no internet to go and complain on. This is where the computer game magazines earned their corn. Their job was to tell you which games were rubbish and best avoided. Colin Ritman reads Crash magazine (this was for Spectrum users - Commodore 64 users had ZZAP!64). Colin's name is a nod to

Jon Ritman - a famous programmer of the era responsible for games like the isometric puzzle classic Head Over Heels.

Jeff Minter makes a cameo in Bandersnatch as Jerome F. Davies, the author of the book that Stefan is adapting into a game. Jeff Minter is a real life game designer who become famous for crazy llama themed shoot 'em ups in the 1980s. The story in Bandersnatch seems influenced by quantum physics. Hugh Everett III (1930–1982) was the first physicist who proposed the many-worlds interpretation (MWI) of quantum physics, which he termed his "relative state" formulation. The theory suggests there are a very large — perhaps infinite — number of universes where parallel versions of our world might exist. As ever with Black Mirror the casting is excellent. Will Poulter steals the show as the nerdy but charismatic Colin Ritman and Craig Parkinson is very good as Stefan's worried father. Fionn Whitehead, who is probably best known for his lead role in Christopher Nolan's Dunkirk, is also reasonably well cast as the troubled Stefan. I must say, you certainly sense Stefan's frustration when his computer keeps crashing before he can finish the game! There are a multitude of different endings and pathways in Bandersnatch although quite often you don't really feel like you are in full control (which, as we mentioned earlier, might have been the point). Stefan becomes convinced he is being controlled too - which he is, by us the viewer! There is no happy ending for Stefan in this story - which is in the spirit of Black Mirror at least.

While this episode is an interesting experiment the actual story in Bandersnatch is never terribly compelling and the interactive narrative does lead to some unavoidable frustration in the end. Really, for this type of experimental interactive episode you probably needed a stronger and more interesting story because watching Stefan slowly get ever more doolally and paranoid simply becomes a drag in the end. The best stuff in this episode is the actual computer game stuff (like the kid who reviews games on television)_ but there simply aren't enough of these scenes. i would have liked to see more the game Stefan was designing and the story lean more into the games scene of this era (as opposed to primarily being a story about mental disintegration). The forgotten 1983 anthology horror film Nightmares has an enjoyably daft segment called The Bishop of Battle where a teenager learns that a video arcade game has a mysterious thirteenth level - which leads to much danger and some hokey Tron style effects. Ultimately I'd rather watch The Bishop of Battle than Bandersnatch because Bandersnatch - even for Black Mirror - is just too depressing for its own good. Bandersnatch can't be faulted for ambition and it is laudable to see Black Mirror trying to do something completely different but this would have to go down as an interesting but flawed experiment rather than a great episode in its own right. You really needed a better story for an interactive episode than the one on offer here.

SERIES 5 (2019)

STRIKING VIPERS

(Directed by Owen Harris, Written by Charlie Brooker)

SYNOPSIS - Danny Parker (Anthony Mackie) and Karl Houghton (Yahya Abdul-Mateen II) are two old friends who lost touch for a number of years. They meet up again at a family barbecue and Karl gives Danny a video game as a birthday present. It's the latest version of Striking Vipers - a Tekken/Mortal Kombat style game the two used to play together when they were younger. The latest version of Striking Vipers is a virtual reality game where you plug yourself into the action and lay comatose as you play as whatever character you've selected. Danny and Karl's characters Lance and Roxette begin by fighting in the game but at some juncture they kiss and have sex. The game replicates the sensations of combat but it clearly does a lot more than that and is basically virtual reality sex technology - if that is how one chooses to use it. This is exactly how Danny and Karl wind up using it and they become addicted to the sex sessions they have through the game. It begins to affect Danny's marriage and his wife Theo (Nicole Beharie) is unaware of his hobby. Danny decides he will have to stop these Striking Viper sessions with Karl but Karl is not happy about this...

REVIEW - Series five of Black Mirror only consisted of three episodes and none of them are what you would say was the show anywhere near its best. This is comfortably the most forgettable season of the show and none of the three episodes are especially memorable - quite the opposite. This is a mediocre triumvirate of stories. If season five was someone's introduction to Black Mirror it probably wouldn't encourage them to stick with the show and explore the rest of the catalogue. Charlie Brooker said it was a choice between giving people a shorter three episode season five or making them wait a long time for a six episode season so he chose the former rather than the latter. In hindsight they might have been better off holding off season five until they had some better scripts because all the stories in this truncated season feel underwhelming and like Black Mirror operating in second gear. All three of the stories in season five would be the weak link or something close to that in other seasons of Black Mirror. Our opening story Striking Vipers is not the most memorable episode of Black Mirror and becomes something of a drag to get through in the end. This is one of those stories where you could easily have chopped some material out and told the basic story in half an hour. There is something oddly bland and mainstream about Striking Vipers - despite the video game sex antics.

Striking Vipers is about male bonding, sexuality, boredom, marriage and trying to work out who you are. The two friends becoming addicted to this game (to the detriment of Danny's marriage) has some obvious parallels with porn addiction. If one is neglecting a partner to watch porn all night is this akin to cheating? The same question can be posed in relation to Danny and Karl playing Striking Vipers all the time while Danny's wife sleeps upstairs. The strange situation that Danny and Karl find themselves in is also analogous to having an affair - though they are conducting this 'affair' online rather than in the real world. Karl tells Danny that he has tried 'virtual sex' with other players and characters but nothing is ever the same. It is only playing Striking Vipers with Danny that gives him this feeling. Karl is therefore completely addicted to the game. It has become like a drug to him. I suppose one could venture a possible subtext about video game addiction in general - which can be a thing. Charlie Brooker said this episode was inspired by the Tekken sessions him and his male friends had in the 1990s. It struck Brooker that there was something faintly homoerotic about a group of men bonding over a game where they wrestle and punch one another! The subtext here could read as a commentary on how people find it much easier to live out their fantasies on screens than actually engage with the real world (which requires a lot more effort than just sitting in your bedroom playing a game or chatting online).

The question that Danny and Karl have to ask themselves is whether their sexual chemistry is confined to Striking Vipers or a carry over from hidden feelings they have in the real world. Are they both gay? When they put this to the test though and kiss in real life there is nothing there at all. No attraction or chemistry. So it was purely the game. They can't seem to find anything in the real world (or indeed the online world) that is as addictive or exciting as their Striking Vipers sessions. So this episode has a big theme about the tension between fantasy and reality. Nothing can replicate Striking Vipers but constantly playing this game is going to have harmful consequences on their lives. The ultimate message in this episode seems hardly worth the wait. The moral of Striking Vipers seems to be find a leisure pursuit balance and be more honest with your wife. That's about it. The story and themes in this episodes are never really interesting enough to sustain a sixty minute story and the characters themselves are rather dull. Striking Vipers seems to take an age to get going too and feels padded beyond its natural duration.

The game sequences are nicely done though and visually striking - riffing on a number of real games like Mortal Kombat and Street Fighter. If you've played any number of these fighting games you'll know what to expect. Health bars, leg sweeps, punching, special moves and attacks, and plenty of bone-crunching violence. Mortal Kombat was one of the games which helped establish the trope in fighting games where your opponent can be rendered vulnerable and inert and THEN finished off in this weakened state with a spectacular final flourish - like, foe example, ripping their heart out of their chest! It is certainly odd in this episode that a Street Fighter style fighting game gives you the option of having realistic sex with whoever you are playing against! Why even bother including the fighting component? I suppose we can perhaps suggest the Striking Vipers tech might have started life as some sort of virtual reality sex experience. Maybe in the near future world depicted here all games, be it Doom or Super Mario, give you the option of having sex in the game! You'd definitely want to keep Striking Vipers away from curious minors. This angle to the technology in Striking Vipers is never really explained. The ending has Danny coming clean to his wife Theo about his virtual reality sex sessions in Striking Vipers. They make a pact. Danny and Karl are allowed to play the game at certain times and Theo is allowed to go to bars, take off her wedding ring and pick up men. What? That is genuinely the ending.

I did ultimately struggle with Striking Vipers and never felt fully engaged or engrossed in the story. The middling user scores this episode accrued tends to conform its status as one of the less impressive episodes of the show. The main problem with this episode, which is basically an exploration of masculinity. lust, monogamy and male bonding, is that the story is never as interesting as Charlie Brooker thinks it is. One is never entirely convinced that the core premise of Striking Vipers is strong enough to justify turning it into a Black Mirror episode. Once the twist of the two men having sex in the game is first shown it feels as if Striking Vipers isn't quite sure where to go next. It feels like the story has played its big gimmick and has nowhere else to go. So you get the impression that Brooker came up with this concept of two straight friends using a computer game through which to have virtual sex but didn't really know how to build a bigger story out of that. Now, this is not to say that everyone was as lukewarm about Striking Vipers as I was. Some people enjoyed this episode much and got more out of it than me - which is fine because Black mirror, as we have mentioned, is one of those shows where it is difficult to get a clear consensus on episodes. I liked Metalhead more than most people seemed to. We all have episodes we like and episodes that we struggled with.

One thing you can't fault in Striking Vipers is the acting with good performances by the leads. This episode also has plenty of humour - like when Karl says he had sex with a polar bear in a game in an attempt to forget Danny but it wasn't the same. This then would presumably qualify as a sly (or not so sly) White Bear reference. Striking Vipers has an interesting concept at the heart of the story but for me this concept is not sufficient in and of itself to fuel a fairly long episode of Black Mirror. When you factor in my lack of investment in the characters then striking Vipers was an episode that washed over me for the large part and didn't really grab me in the way that Black Mirror can at its very best. This is one of those Black Mirror episodes that I always struggle to remember much about - save for the sex twist in the fighting game. And that is the main problem with Striking Vipers. When you get past the early twist there isn't really much left to keep the momentum and interest going.

SMITHEREENS

(Directed by James Hawes, Written by Charlie Brooker)

SYNOPSIS - Chris Gillhaney (Andrew Scott) is a rideshare driver in London who kidnaps an intern named Jaden (Damson Idris) from a social media company called Smithereen. Chris ends up attracting the attention of the police and eventually crashes the car into a field in a rural spot. Police snipers are called in and a hostage situation develops. Chris, who is in contact with the police by phone in his car, demands to speak to the Smithereen CEO Billy Bauer (Topher Grace) - who is away at a meditation retreat. Why is Chris so obsessed with Smithereen and why does he wish to speak to the CEO?

REVIEW - Smithereens is the best of the three episodes in series five but that's not saying an awful lot because this is still pretty mediocre stuff by the usual standards of Black Mirror. Smithereens feels way too long at 71 minutes (one suspects an extra long episode was put in here in an attempt to mitigate the fact there are only three episodes in season five) and like Striking Vipers is another episode that becomes something of a slog to get through in the end. A hostage drama in a field is not exactly the most exciting of Black Mirror stories and hostage dramas in general have been done to death in films and television over the years so Smithereens can't help but come across as too familiar for its own good. The thing which anchors this episode and makes it somewhat more watchable than it might otherwise have been is the excellent performance by Andrew Scott as Chris. It's a shame really that Scott didn't get a better episode to appear in because he's acting his socks off here but is stuck in one of those unmemorable Black Mirror stories where you don't really remember much about it afterwards. In terms of the basic premise there is little in this episode to hook the viewer or keep us gripped. Damson Idris, like Scott, is also very good as the kidnapped intern. Both of these actors deserved a better story to be in. Some of the supporting cast in this episode are a bit hit or miss though and the writing isn't the best. The police stuff in this episode doesn't always feel terribly convincing. I can't be the only person to have found the police snipers comical in their incompetence.

On the surface Smithereens feels like a parody of the broad general stereotype of a Black Mirror story. We learn at the end that Chris holds himself responsible for the car accident which killed his fiancée. The accident occurred because he was distracted and checking a Smithereen social media notification while driving. This twist in this episode feels like a tongue-in-cheek response by Charlie Brooker to the broadest most superficial perception of the show (which is something like mobile phones = bad things will happen) but it would be wrong to focus on this twist (which appears to be stating the bleeding obvious - don't use your phone while driving!) as the true message of Smithereens. The real message comes at the end where people are milling about at the hostage location and filming everything on their phones like mindless zombies. Once the situation ends these people will drift off and probably forget they ever filmed this stuff in the first place. Chris, in his last hours, has been reduced to a few random images on tiny screen. His plight and life has been made to seem trivial by technology. Smithereens does though have a commentary on the fiendishly addictive nature of social media and checking for messages. I write this as someone with no social media at all but I have seen the hold it has over people as they blankly wander down the street eyes glued to their phone.

Charlie Brooker said he has experienced social media addiction himself in the past where literally the first thing he would do in the morning was look at Twitter. This is probably not a great state of affairs to find yourself in because the online world isn't the be all and end all and can be a toxic place to spend too much time in. You would probably be in a healthier state of mind if you avoided social media and the news in general. This would require unplugging yourself from the conversation hub - something many people could not bring themselves to do. One interesting aspect to this episode is that the social media company turn out to be much better at collecting information about Chris than the police - which is all too realistic. The big tech corporations are sitting on a ton of information about everyone and are often loath to divulge that information - even in criminal cases. Information is a form of power and the corporations are nothing if not obsessed with becoming even more powerful. We now live in a world where huge corporations seem to be as powerful as governments and act as if the normal laws of business (like paying a fair share of tax in the nations where they do commerce and make money) don't apply to them.

We see (in a rather grim scene) Chris have sex with Hayley (Amanda Drew) at the start of Smithereens. Hayley is a member of a therapy group he attends. Hayley's daughter committed suicide but Hayley can't access the social media and email accounts of her late daughter's laptop to look for clues on why she might have taken her life. At the end of the episode Chris persuades the Smithereen CEO to give Hayley access to her daughter's laptop accounts. Chris has had one tangible success then at the end. It wasn't all completely in vain. Brooker, wisely perhaps, doesn't make the Smithereen CEO Billy Bauer a panto villain in this episode. Billy comes across as fairly oblivious and detached from his company. He's more like a hippy who is tired of corporate life rather than some Bezos style Bond villain. Billy clearly has regrets about the 'monster' he helped to create and would happily leave the boardroom behind and retire to a shack on the beach. Topher Grace doesn't have a huge amount to do in this episode as the CEO but he's good in what scenes he has. There is though something oddly vague and undercooked about Smithereens. There isn't an impressive or interesting supporting cast and we end up with the fairly dull hostage situation in the field. None of this feels like sufficient material for a seventy minute episode of Black Mirror. In the end Smithereens feels like it is running on fumes trying to stretch this premise out longer than necessary and trying desperately to extract some sort of weight or emotion from the scenario.

The episode entirely rests on the shoulders of Andrew Scott and his strong performance does mitigate the underwhelming nature of this story but it can't completely salvage what is another forgettable season five episode. Much as was the case with Striking Vipers, Smithereens just isn't that interesting as a concept or story and with no satisfying or surprising twist to speak of it all just washes over you. The big problem with season five is that none of the stories are terribly intriguing or interesting. None of them are great ideas for a Black Mirror episode and so the season becomes a slog to get through with no diamond in the rough to rise above everything else and elevate the status of this shortened and disappointing run of episodes. Smithereens feels quite shallow and bland for a Black Mirror episode. While there is nothing wrong with a Black Mirror story about social media and the instinct some have to gawp at tragedy you can't help wishing they had found a more interesting concept through which to explore these themes because a taxi driver having a nervous breakdown and a hostage crisis in a field does not make for the most enthralling viewing experience. Smithereens has its moments and a fine central performance but it would certainly be a stretch to pretend this was one of the better episodes of Black Mirror.

RACHEL, JACK AND ASHLEY TOO

(Directed by Anne Sewitsky, Written by Charlie Brooker)

SYNOPSIS - A teenager named Rachel Goggins (Angourie Rice) lives with her sister Jack (Madison Davenport) and father Kevin (Marc Menchaca). Rachel's mother passed away - which has obviously left a big hole in the family. Rachel is a big fan of the pop star Ashley Ortiz (Miley Cyrus) and on her birthday is given an 'Ashley Too' - which is little robotic AI Ashley doll. Rachel is inseparable from this little talking companion but Jack, irritated by the doll and believing it to not be doing Rachel any good, hides it. Meanwhile, the real Ashley Ortiz is fed up being a manufactured pop star and wants to change her image and write different songs. Her domineering aunt and manager Catherine Ortiz (Susan Pourfar) is not too happy about this at all. Catherine drugs Ashley - which induces a coma. With the aid of a crooked doctor, who extracts Ashley's music from her brainwaves, Catherine 'steals' Asghley's music and continues to release it. Rachel's robotic Ashley doll - it transpires - shares Ashley's consciousness and becomes aware that the pop star is in danger and being exploited. Rachel and Jack set off on a mission to rescue the real Ashley from her wicked aunt...

REVIEW - Rachel, Jack and Ashley Too is (at the time of writing) the second lowest rated episode of Black Mirror on IMDB and it is difficult to muster too much of an argument against that general perception. Charlie Brooker said the genesis of this episode was the basic idea of a popstar trapped in a coma and having music extracted from their head but rather than make this concept a bleak and dark sort of story they decided to make it more of a romp and one of those lighter Black Mirror episodes. Brooker's argument is that if you make every episode of Black Mirror nihilistic and grim then this becomes predictable in the end and makes the show feel samey and as if is constantly mining too narrow a geographical (in an artistic sense) creative well. These decisions are made on a 'whim' according to the mood of the author at time. Brooker said that when this episode was made he was in the mood to do a more optimistic sort of episode that was more Pixar than The Texas Chainsaw Massacre. This explains then why Rachel, Jack and Ashley is (the coma stuff aside) generally lighter and more rompish than a lot of Black Mirror episodes. However, this still it doesn't make the episode any better as a viewing experience.

This episode feels rather muddled in that it begins in vaguely promising fashion with the shy and lonely Rachel becoming reliant on this little AI toy but then somewhere along the line spins off into some daft kids adventure comedy film from the 1980s with the antics of Rachel and Jack trying to infiltrate the mansion and rescue Ashley. It all builds to a pop concert climax which won't be for all tastes. Rachel, Jack and Ashley Too feels like a mish-mash of two or three different ideas, none of which are explored or payed off in a satisfactory way. The end result is underwhelming to say the least. Rachel, Jack and Ashley Too feels more like generic Netflix or Disney slop than prime Black Mirror.

The inspiration for this episode is deceased pop stars being inserted into concerts through old footage or holograms. Charlie Brooker said he finds this sort of thing rather ghoulish and distasteful. So you get the coma bound Ashley being exploited by her aunt. This episode basically functions as a commentary on how record companies and estates seek to continue to make money from a star even when they have died. One could imagine a scenario far in the future where a realistic AI of deceased stars is created to go on tour. Maybe people in the future will be able to watch Elvis in concert.

There is a lot of commentary about celebrities in this episode. How they can find themselves in constrictive management and contract situations where they have no artistic control over their career. We see that Ashley has become a marketing brand with all manner of commercial tie-ins - like the doll. There are probably fast food meals with Ashley's name on them too but it is doubtful she is getting her fair share of the money for all of these endorsements. Singers become cash cows for companies and the more malleable the singer the more the companies like it. We've seen stars like Taylor Swift take personal control of their career but not every singer is powerful or smart enough to do this. Not everyone is Taylor Swift. Ashley Ortiz feels inspired not just by Miley Cyrus but also Britney Spears. Miley Cyrus said herself that her childhood and teen years as Hannah Montana had a negative effect on her mental health. "I think people loved Hannah Montana because Hannah did seem real. And it's because I was under there. I think it got harder when I started touring as both — I toured as Hannah Montana and as myself. Now that I'm older, I realise that's a lot to put on a kid. To have them have to get their makeup done and also balance school. I think what was hard for me was balancing everything. I think that's what's probably a little wrong with me now. I mark that up to doing some extreme damage in my psyche as an adult person."

The acting in this episode is less impressive than the top tier Black Mirror episodes but Angourie Rice does some good work as the shy and lonely Rachel. Miley Cyrus is not the world's greatest thespian and isn't especially charismatic as Ashley in this episode. Another problem with Rachel, Jack and Ashley Too is that at seventy minutes it feels far too long for its own good. it's fine to have longer episodes but this only works if you have a good story that is going to fully engage us throughout. The running times of these season five episodes was clearly intended to be some sort of compensation for only getting three episodes but it is pointless doing an extra long episode unless you have a USS Callister level story that is going to keep us entertained over the longer stretch. If you have a so-so story and an episode that - by the standards of Black Mirror - isn't especially memorable or entertaining then an extended running time merely makes the episode drag in the end and feel like something of a chore to get through. This is where Rod Sering was smart with the Twilight Zone. Apart from one hour long season you are done and dusted with Twilight Zone stories in about half an hour. A number of Black Mirror stories benefit from the length and having more room to breathe but you couldn't really say that Rachel, Jack and Ashley

Too is among them. Rachel, Jack and Ashley Too feels too generic, too lightweight and too forgettable to be an episode of Black Mirror. It is hard to believe that a show which began with episodes like Fifteen Million Merits and White Bear is now making episodes like Rachel, Jack and Ashley Too.

Rachel, Jack and Ashley Too has a rather muddled story which goes nowhere in particular. This episode suffers from a weird tonal shift where it begins in a very Black Mirror sort of way with a sad household and this slightly creepy AI doll but then branches off into a daft kids comedy caper film. Rachel is supposed to be about fifteen in this story so it stretches credibility somewhat that she would become obsessed with the Ashley doll. Would a fifteen year-old still be collecting toys - even one as sophisticated as the Ashley doll? A salient problem with Rachel, Jack and Ashley Too is that it doesn't tell us anything about the pitfalls of fame and celebrity that we didn't already know so does come across as one of those scripts where we are being told the bleeding obvious. The caper stuff at the end feels like a clunky late addition and doesn't chime with the early mood of the piece. Rachel, Jack and Ashley Too has its fans but on the whole you'd have to rank this as one of the weakest episodes in the show and it serves as a disappointing end to what has been a very disappointing season. Season five of Black Mirror feels largely bereft of inspiration and coasting along in second gear. None of these three episodes stick in the memory or ever threaten to crack the Black Mirror top table. By the way, the title of this episode is presumably inspired by the 1980s British comedy film Rita, Sue and Bob Too.

SERIES 6 (2023)

JOAN IS AWFUL

(Directed by Ally Pankiw, Written by Charlie Brooker)

SYNOPSIS - An ordinary woman named Joan Tait (Annie Murphy) is bewildered when she watches television one night and finds a new streaming show called Joan is Awful which appears to be based on her life. Joan is Awful dramatises whatever has happened to the real Joan that day and has the Hollywood actress Salma Hayek in the title role. Having her life depicted in a television show soon begins to have damaging consequences for Joan so she determines to put a stop to it all...

REVIEW - Series six of Black Mirror consisted of five episodes and was thankfully a marked improvement on series five. Some of the episodes in series six are clearly influenced by the horror genre more than is usual for this show and indicate a certain intent to branch out somewhat. Charlie Brooker joked at the time that they could do a horror sister show called Red Mirror - which I'd definitely watch if it ever happened. Joan is Awful is the lightest and most comedic episode in series six and the one that feels the most like a Twilight Zone sort of scenario. Though generally well received by critics this episode does run a fine line though and is a trifle self-satisfied and smug at times with a script that is never quite as funny as it thinks it is. I'm not the biggest fan of frantic farce comedy where everyone keeps shouting and Joan is Awful does threaten to veer into that territory at times. The layers of meta narrative in the script become rather wearisome in the end but generally this episode is competent and interesting and has a central premise that wile hardly original is at least a lot more compelling than anything in season five. Joan is Awful is a variation on the loss of identity theme (which is well worn in anthology shows) and somewhat evokes the Twilight Zone episode A World of Difference where a businessman is bewildered to be told he is not a businessman at all but merely a character in a television show. Joan is Awful does though dig down deep in the meta levels with nothing at all as it seems and Joan having to team up with Salma Hayek to put a stop to the show.

Annie Murphy and Salma Hayek give unrestrained performances in this episode but that's in keeping with the tone of the piece and both of these actors are very good. The meta element is heightened by characters being played by different actors as the meta layers pile up. It is revealed that 'Streamberry' (the Netflix type streamer who make Joan is Awful) uses a quantum computer and CGI and through social media data can then construct a television show based on what happened to Joan that day. So you can detect a theme about the image rights of celebrities in this story. Joan literally loses the rights to her own life in this story. But can she, so to speak, seize back the narrative? Salma Hayek isn't even in the show Joan is Awful - despite being the lead. She has merely signed her likeness away. If this sort of technology ever became real it would probably be heaven for film companies because they could have whoever they wanted as the lead of a show without having to put up with the whims and demands of an actual person! In order to put a stop to the show based on her life Joan decides to take extreme measures - like defecate in a church. They surely won't put that in the show will they? This is quite a clever idea by Joan because she knows that Salma Hayek won't be too happy about seeing her likeness depicted in such a tasteless scene and will kick up a fuss with Streamberry.

So in the end Joan eventually teams up with Salma Hayek to take down the Streamberry computer - which leads to some big revelations about the true nature of reality. Joan is Awful is one of those Black Mirror episodes with a happy ending and along with the comedic tone this makes it one of the lighter episodes Brooker has written. As far as the lighter episodes go though this is a perfectly decent and watchable one. The story in Joan is Awful obviously touches on the real life phenomenon of technology now being able to mimic real people. We've seen, for example, deceased actors like Peter Cushing and Ian Holm put in new films through technology and this technology is becoming more sophisticated all the time so where will it end? There might come a time when studios don't even need actors. A number of celebrities have (obviously without their permission) been used as 'deepfakes' by scammers for hoax advertising. This sort of stuff is like a Black Mirror story only real. There is a nice joke in this episode where it is explained that the title Joan is Awful comes from algorithms deducing that people respond more to negative things. If the show was called Joan is Nice or Joan is Lovely it wouldn't have got so many viewers. One could construe that as a little meta comment on Black Mirror - where the bleak dystopia episodes generally (San Junipero aside perhaps) tend to be the most celebrated and memorable.

Joan is Awful also has an obvious theme about the privacy of data - which is highly relevant in our own society. Streamberry are exploiting the data they have accrued on Joan for financial reasons without even asking for consent. There are a number of cameos in Joan is Awful and Michael Cera pops up near the end as a technician. This episode pulls that old Black Mirror trick of having reality exposed as a simulation and becomes increasingly knotty as it winds towards a conclusion. When you strip everything back though you have a concept that probably didn't need a sixty minute running time (Rod Serling could have adapted this story in thirty minutes without too much trouble) and the frantic comedic tone often makes this less compelling than the better (and darker) episodes of Black Mirror. Joan is Awful is decent enough for what it is and a solid enough comedic entry but you wouldn't put this anywhere near the Black Mirror premier league when it comes to the very best episodes in the show. What helps a lot though is that there are aren't really any other episodes in this lighter and more comedic vein in season six so its function (as a change of pace) becomes more evident and perhaps even necessary. Season six is quite dark and horror-centric as an overall block of stories so having something like Joan is Awful in here too just helps to break things up and you at least one episode with more of a humorous slant.

Joan is Awful is not my favourite type of Black Mirror story with the meta comedy and over the top performances but it's fine for what it is and does have some genuine Black Mirror residue with the technology themes. There are some sly jokes and while not amazingly funny it breezes along without dangerously threatening to outstay its welcome too much. You could argue that this episode is a trifle too twisty for its own good in the end but it generally works well enough as a comic riff on privacy, celebrity, image rights and the human instinct to carp and dwell on the negative rather than the positive. Joan is Awful is better than any of the three season five episodes and although not what you would call a classic episode of Black Mirror it is a solid enough start for season six.

LOCH HENRY

(Directed by Sam MIller, Written by Charlie Brooker)

SYNOPSIS - A young man named Davis McCardle (Samuel Blenkin) travels back to his childhood home of Loch Henry in Scotland to stay with his mother Janet (Monica Dolan). His American girlfriend Pia Koreshi (Myha'la Herrold) is with him. Davis wants to show Pia where he grew up. He's also mulling over making a documentary about conservation in the area. Davis and Pia visit the only pub left open in the town - which is run by his old friend Stuart King (Daniel Portman). Pia learns that tourists tend to stay away from Loch Henry because of a notorious serial killer case in the 1990s. A local man named Iain Adair (Tom Crowhurst) murdered a number of tourists at his cottage and then killed himself and his family. Kenneth McCardle, the late father of Davis, was a police officer at the time and went to arrest Adair - but was then shot and never recovered from his injuries. This is the general gist of the local true crime story as told to Pia. But is it the truth?

REVIEW - Loch Henry is one of the more overt horror episodes of Black Mirror and takes a degree of inspiration from The Blair Witch Project with its focus on old technology and old mysteries slowly coming into focus. There are some scenes in here akin to found footage horror films so one can clearly see some of the influences on this story. The biggest influence on Loch Henry though is the explosion of the 'true crime' genre. You literally can't go a week without some new crime documentary appearing on television and the more macabre and strange the crimes the more people are interested. Television dramas based on notorious killers (like the drama Des based on Dennis Nilsen) can get huge viewing figures. There have been endless biopics about serial killers in film and on television and countless films that take inspiration from real life killers. Netflix have produced high profile dramas on Bundy and Dahmer. Ed Gein inspired the Texas Chainsaw Massacre, Psycho, The Silence of the Lambs, Deranged, In the Light of the Moon (which stars Steve Railsback as Gein). 1974's Deranged stars Roberts Blossom as Ezra Cobb (Cobb is clearly based on Gein), a nutty rural chap who exhumes his mother and begins abducting and killing local women.

We are fascinated by the likes of Jeffrey Dahmer, Ted Bundy, Fred, West and Dennis Nilsen because their crimes are unfathomable. True crime is big business with 'murder tours', podcasts, books, and even memorabilia (or 'murderabilia' as it tends to be known) websites where you can buy things which once belonged to a famous serial killer. True crime 'collectibles' websites have all manner of stuff you can buy. For example, fancy owning a polaroid photograph of Arthur Shawcross for $275? No, me neither. A true crime collectible site put up for sale an Ambrosia chocolate factory pay check made out to Jeffrey Dahmer. Dahmer's signature is on the back. The price you'd have to pay to own this pay check? $15,000! There are websites and books devoted to what serial killers had as their last meal on death row before being executed. John Wayne Gacy, who murdered 33 teenage boys and young men between 1972 and 1978, requested 12 fried shrimp, a bucket of original recipe KFC, French fries, and strawberries. We know all this trivia because we are strangely obsessed with true crime monsters. If you want to write a book then true crime is as good a bet as any for your subject because there is always a market for this stuff. And you have weird phenomena too like hybristophilia. Hybristophilia is sometimes referred to as Bonnie and Clyde syndrome. It is this condition which makes women write to serial killers in prison. No matter how awful the killer is, you can guarantee that killer has received fan mail and that there are probably women out there who would be perfectly willing to meet them and, in some cases, even marry them.

Loch Henry suggests there is something unavoidably ghoulish and distasteful about the true crime genre where these depraved killers become celebrities and the victims are sometimes completely forgotten. Everyone has heard of Ted Bundy but how many people could name even a few of his victims? And there is truth in Loch Henry's message. It is distasteful because when you boil it down the true crime genre is basically making money off the back of tragedy and real life misery. But there is something morbidly compelling about this genre which draws us in. I can't claim any moral high ground on this because I watch true crime documentaries myself and have probably read more about famous serial killers than is good for me. Our enduring fascination with serial killers stems from the fact that they are completely unfathomable and alien to us. We are constrained and guided in our actions by compassion, guilt, remorse, empathy, and kindness. Most of us are very squeamish. Serial killers are not constrained by any of these normal human emotions. They rape, torture, kill, cut up bodies, and commit the most gruesome acts as if it was the most natural thing in the world.

In the plot of Loch Henry, a reluctant Davis is eventually persuaded to make a true crime documentary about the local killer Iain Adair by Pia. So instead of a conservation documentary he has joined the growing true crime market - which makes Davis uncomfortable. The documentary is also unavoidably going to open up some old wounds concerning his father. His friend Stuart (played by no lesser figure than Podrick from Game of Thrones) is all for the documentary because he believes the exposure will draw visitors to the town and boost takings at the pub. There's a slight potential weakness here in the story because one might have assumed that the grisly legend of Iain Adair would have drawn some true crime tourists into the town rather than drive them away. Adair would have made Loch Henry famous - as opposed to some Silent Hill type of place that everyone avoided like the plague. And these true crime tourists would definitely have stopped off at the pub. The story ignores this though and portrays Loch Henry as a ghost town where the local serial killer history stops anyone from wanting to visit (presumably because they fear they might get murdered - which doesn't make much sense because Adair is dead).

The scenes where the Adair cottage is explored are enjoyably found footage and Loch Henry has plenty of mystery and atmosphere as a story. Stuart's father Richard (John Hannah) is used as a red herring in the narrative. Richard seems to know more about Adair then he has thus far let on so we wonder if he might have been involved in the murders. What makes this enjoyable as a crime episode is that it's quite seedy and grim in places so is something different from the Nordic Noir inspired Black Mirror episodes. The big twist is that it was the parents of Davis who were the killers. Kenneth and Janet tortured, murdered and filmed the victims and Adair was it seems little more than a bystander under the thumb of these two monsters. Kenneth murdered the Adair family and then gave himself a gunshot injury to create the fictitious tale that was passed down - that of Ian being the depraved killer and Kenneth the dutiful brave local copper who stopped him. Davis is faced with a horrible truth at the end of this story. His seemingly kind and normal parents were actually akin to Fred and Rose West.

That's a great moment in this episode when Pia is left alone with Janet after Davis is injured in a crash. Janet seems much like any other mother. She has Bergerac VHS tapes on the shelf and makes a good shepherd's pie. Pia discovers a shocking secret on a Bergerac tape. These are snuff films. Janet has kept the footage of the victims they killed. In a dungeon we see Kenneth declare 'here comes the mistress' before Janet appears wearing a mask and PVC and carrying a drill. Janet is Rose West from hell. Pia flees but trips in a stream and dies. Janet (who doesn't know Pia died) commits suicide. At the end we see David picking up awards for his documentary. Everyone involved is thrilled - except Davis. The success is empty and meaningless. His girlfriend died and his parents were exposed as West style serial killers. His mother has committed suicide. The ending has a nice irony because the main criticism of true crime is that it is basically profiting from the tragedies of others. Davis is now experiencing both of these tangents. He is profiting from true crime but the tragedy he has 'exploited' is one that involved his own family. He is therefore both profiteer and victim. So the success and money he has gained from the documentary is meaningless because it came at great personal cost.

Loch Henry is more Hammer House of Horror/Hammer House of Mystery and Suspense than Twilight Zone but that's fine by me and this episode is highly watchable and compelling. Loch Henry, one might argue, is rather underrated in the Black Mirror collection because it does exactly what it sets out to do and works very well as a crime thriller with found footage horror film influences. The plot in this episode doesn't have airtight logic but Loch Henry is scary in places and the central mystery is enough to keep one engaged and interested. I have seen Loch Henry ranked quite low in some subjective Black

Mirror rankings but I don't quite understand this myself because this is an interesting and entertaining horror themed episode on the whole. The technology theme is this episode is somewhat vague so one could perhaps argue that it doesn't feel a lot like a Black Mirror episode but for what it is Loch Henry is watchable and interesting and a very solid episode indeed with some enjoyably dark and twisted flourishes.

BEYOND THE SEA

(Directed by John Crowley, Written by Charlie Brooker)

SYNOPSIS - In an alternate 1969, astronauts, Cliff (Aaron Paul) and David (Josh Hartnett) are on a six year mission together on a small space station in orbit. The two men can't leave the station but they can temporarily transfer their consciousness to artificial versions of themselves back on Earth. This technology allows Cliff and David to spend time with their families and not miss out on their children growing up. Tragedy strikes though when David's consciousness is on Earth. There is a home invasion by some nutty cult group who believe artificial bodies are an abomination. The cult group murder David's family and then destroy his artificial body - which was one of a kind. Back on the station in his human body, David is inconsolable. In an attempt to help, Cliff agrees with his wife Lana (Kate Mara) that David should be allowed to transfer his consciousness to Cliff's replica body so that he can walk in the forest and have some time alone. David is then permitted to transfer himself to Cliff's clone on Earth for an hour a week so he can do some painting and get away from the station. David begins to have feelings for Cliff's wife though and as he's in a duplicate of Cliff's body Lana, who is lonely, can't help but have some feelings in return...

REVIEW - Beyond the Sea is basically a story about isolation and the need for human connections. It turns into this strange and bleak love triangle that most assuredly does not have a happy ending. Charlie Brooker apparently wrote this episode during the pandemic and one can see how that is woven into the story. Beyond the Sea has some thematic connections to the Twilight Zone episodes Where is Everybody? and The Lonely - which are both about how isolation can sap the soul. This episode, with its space station backdrop, is more overtly science fiction than a lot of Black Mirror episodes and while this is fun the episode has some glacial pacing which won't be everyone's cup of tea. The cult leader Kappa (Rory Culkin) who murders David's family is clearly based on Charles Manson - which is one explanation for why this episode is set in 1969. In 1969, Sharon Tate was an actress who had appeared in films like The Fearless Vampire Killers and Valley of the Dolls. At 26 years of age, Sharon Tate seemed destined to become a huge star. Alas though, fate was to intervene in horrific fashion. On August 8, 1969, Sharon Tate, who was nine months pregnant, was entertaining some friends at her Hollywood home. Her husband Roman Polanski was away in London making a film. Tate and her friends were subject to one of the most evil and infamous home invasions in history thanks to the orders of the nutty but charismatic cult leader Charles Manson.

Manson had sent four of his 'followers' - Linda Kasabian, Tex Watson, Susan Atkins, and Patricia "Katie" Krenwinkel - to go and murder Tate. Tate's friends Jay Sebring, Wojciech Frykowski, and Abigail Folger, who were unfortunate enough to be in the house that night, were also killed. The Manson cult members had cut the phone lines before they climbed over the walls to the property. Sharon Tate was stabbed nearly twenty times. There were stab wounds from her head to her feet. The word 'pig' was scrawled on a door in her blood. This was a horrific attack on innocent people. The victims were beaten, hung, stabbed, shot, and suffered a dreadful ordeal. Charles Manson and three of the assailants were all sentenced to life in prison for this senseless and tragic act of violence. Manson wasn't actually present at the murders but he had issued the instructions and egged on his brainwashed followers to commit these crimes. Manson's plan was to commit horrific crimes to blame on black Americans to incite a race war. This was a plan he named Helter Skelter. Needless to say, Manson was completely crazy.

The author Joan Didion wrote of the Sharon Tate murders - "Many people I know in Los Angeles believe that the Sixties ended abruptly on August 9, 1969, ended at the exact moment when word of the murders on Cielo Drive travelled like brushfire through the community, and in a sense this is true." The murder of Sharon Tate was one of the most brutal and shocking in Hollywood history. Beyond the Sea alludes to Manson murders in that you have this time of great optimism. The space programme is flourishing and a retro future world has arrived. But then Kappa arrives on the scene and destroys David's world. All that progress and optimism suddenly counts for nothing as far as David is concerned. David's life was taken from him but he is given a window into Cliff's life when he spends time with Cliff's family through the artificial duplicate. The general gist of this story is that David was a loving and attentive husband and father whereas Clif is a more unemotional and aloof sort of man. David becomes increasingly twisted by his sense that Cliff doesn't deserve the family he has and doesn't give them enough attention. David is given a means to sort of steal Cliff's life and he's troubled enough to exploit that.

David begins to take advantage of being in Cliff's likeness by trying to woo Cliff's wife Lana. It builds to a bleak climax where David murders Cliff's family and the two men are left alone on the space station - now in the same boat both literally and emotionally. The station needs two astronauts to function so neither can leave. If Cliff murdered David in revenge he would die too. Beyond the Sea is impeccably acted by the three leads. The space station scenes are atmospheric and somewhat reminiscent of the Duncan Jones film Moon. Moon is an inventive bargain basement sci-fi movie that won rave reviews and proved that you don't need a huge budget and fancy special effects to make an interesting film. The film takes place in a lunar base on the moon. Sam Bell (Sam Rockwell) is on a solo three year moon mission mining helium-3. The company behind this operation had deduced that they can save a lot of money with just a single employee in charge. Beyond the Sea is a lot more claustrophobia than Moon though due to the constrictive nature of the space station. You would definitely get cabin fever if you couldn't occasionally transfer to an artificial body on Earth for some shore leave.

The retro future design of this episode is excellent. I gather that Cliff's house was depicted by a house in Whitstable - which is a town I used to live in myself. This is generally a solid episode but it does have one big problem. At eighty minutes this episode is another which is simply too long for its own good. The story is never quite compelling enough to justify a near feature length running time so Beyond the sea - which is a very slow burn sort of episode more about character and atmosphere than twists or action - does tend to drag somewhat in the end. There is no reason why this couldn't have been a slightly shorter episode and in that format it might have worked better. You would describe Beyond the Sea as solid rather than a classic Black Mirror episode. The ending is sort of predictable and the pacing does stretch one's patience at times but Beyond the Sea does get a big boost from the lead actors and the creeping sense of doom and bleakness of this tale does ultimately make it feel very Black Mirror in spirit. This is a good episode but not a terribly exciting or surprising one and so Beyond the Sea, as far as Black Mirror goes, tends to sit somewhere in the middle of the pack overall. Beyond the Sea is interesting and well made but it isn't something you would immediately rush back to if you were doing a Black Mirror marathon.

MAZEY DAY

(Directed by Uta Briesewitz, Written by Charlie Brooker)

SYNOPSIS - The year is 2006. Paparazzi photographer Bo (Zazie Beetz) is becoming tired plying her sleazy trade where she must trail celebrities and get evidence of muck, scandal or infidelity to sell to the tabloid rags. Bo quits but soon finds that having no money is not ideal because she can't pay the rent. There is a possible solution to her financial woes though. A famous Hollywood actress named Mazey Day (Clara Rugaard) quit a film in mysterious circumstances and hasn't been seen in public since. Mazey has become more elusive than Greta Garbo or J.D Salinger. A photograph of the reclusive Mazey Day would therefore be worth an awful lot of money ($30,000 to be precise) if one could be secured. Through her connections and own detective skills, Bo believes she might be able to track down Mazy Day's whereabouts and take a photograph of this vanished and enigmatic star...

REVIEW - Mazey Day is by far the lowest rated episode of Black Mirror on IMDB with (at the time of writing) a dismal 5.3 out of ten. This is also the shortest episode in the series and runs to 43 minutes in total. Why did this episode suffer such a tepid reaction? There are a number of factors which might help explain that. The story has no Black Mirror bleak dystopia technology trappings and the paparazzi theme feels like old hat and something that has already been done better elsewhere (watch the film Nightcrawler). The game has moved on these days when it comes to this type of story. Celebrities today are now more worried about naked pictures of them ending up in the cloud or deepfake porn than dodging paparazzi at hotels. Mazey Day is set in 2006 because in our smartphone festooned modern world everyone is a potential paparazzi who can film or photograph celebrities. It is no longer a unique and rarefied field. Charlie Brooker, being British, would have noticed the press hounding of (late) celebrities like Amy Winehouse, Caroline Flack and Princess Diana by a heartless media pack and so you get these sorts of themes woven into the story.

Mazey Day also obviously works as an analogue for American celebrities too like Britney Spears and Paris Hilton - who suffered more than their fair share of press intrusion. The salient problem in Mazey Day is that the twist comes across as daft and not exactly dripping in Black Mirror residue. It feels like one of those twists were the sole purpose was to whip the rug out from under the viewer. Once the twist is activated though Mazey Day has nowhere to go as a story and weakly fizzles out. The twist is that Mazey Day has become a werewolf. The reason she quit the film is that she, while high on magic mushrooms, went out to get cigarettes and ran into a werewolf on a country road and then got bitten. So she was hidden away like a celebrity going through rehab - when in fact she is a werewolf and must be chained up when there is a full moon. This story is maybe a half-decent idea for a half-hour episode of Tales from the Darkside but it isn't a tremendously good fit for an episode of Black Mirror. So this is one of those episodes which makes us ponder the remit of the show. Black Mirror is not confined to any single tone but it did establish itself with bleak dystopia tales about technology with some crazy twists. A story about a secretive celebrity who turns out to be a werewolf feels as if it has drifted out of the Black Mirror remit into something completely different. This is really a Tales from the Crypt episode but alas not a very good Tales from the Crypt episode.

Of the three horror episodes in series six, Loch Henry worked much better than Mazey Day because it had a technology theme (which riffed on found footage horror) and also more interesting things to say about the media. Demon 79 (which is up next) also worked better than Mazey Day as a horror yarn because it had more charismatic leads and a more compelling story. In comparison to these stories Mazey Day can't help but come off as something of a dud. Bo and her press cohorts eventually find Mazy chained to a cabin bed and then the episode becomes a werewolf caper in the last act with the climax taking place in a diner. Bo eventually shoots Mazy (who has reverted to human form) at Mazey's request but Bo makes sure to take a photograph to sell while she is doing this. It's a cynical coda with some Black Mirror residue but it isn't enough to save the episode. When you watch this episode for the first time you presume that Mazey has been kidnapped by some crazy Hollywood cult or something along those lines but this obviously doesn't turn out to be the case. While the story here does subvert any expectations we might have (I can't believe too many people would have accurately predicted the werewolf twist with no prior knowledge of this episode) it doesn't really cut the mustard as a big reveal and foundation for the last act.

The problem with Mazey Day is that the werewolf twist can't help but feel underwhelming. The concept of a Hollywood actor going missing and being tracked down by a photographer could have worked quite well with a more interesting and novel twist but Mazey Day's (ahem) transformation into a werewolf caper isn't tremendously satisfying. If you want a werewolf story there are plenty of films out there you'd probably be better off watching instead. Go and watch The Beast Must Die, Silver Bullet, An American Werewolf in London, Ginger Snaps or any number of werewolf films. You'll probably have a better time with them than you would with Mazey Day. Mazey Day doesn't have enough atmosphere or suspense to really work as a horror episode so it comes off as this tonally confusing paparazzi satire which suddenly plunges us into a fairly mediocre werewolf yarn. Other anthology television shows have also done better werewolf stories too than the one you get in Mazey Day. One thinks of Children of the Full Moon in Hammer House of Horror or even Werewolf Concerto in Tales from the Crypt. So the twist is Mazey day feels plucked from nowhere and not terribly novel or interesting.

The actual mystery in the early parts of the episode of Bo looking for Mazey are mildly intriguing but these paparazzi characters are never as interesting or convincing as the script needs them to be for the story to flourish. Early on in this episode we see Bo confronted by an unfaithful celebrity she has tracked down to a hotel. He implores her not to divulge the information she has gleaned but Bo ignores him and drives away with her (photographic) bounty. A story about this sort of thing (where perhaps a celebrity became vengeful towards Bo) would probably have been more interesting than a werewolf caper that merely has a few obvious jabs at a profession which barely exists anymore. This is one of those Black Mirror episodes where you don't really remember much about the characters afterwards. The characters and story feel undercooked and in need of more time in the oven. I don't think Mazey Day is quite as terrible as some of the reviews would suggest but I wouldn't pretend it is much good either. Ultimately this is a forgettable sort of episode that doesn't feel very much like Black Mirror. It's a shame really because season six is generally interesting and pretty good so Mazey day can't help but lower the batting average somewhat and feel like a disappointment when contrasted with the other episodes in this season. One of the problems with Mazey Day is that once the big twist is revealed the script doesn't quite seem to know what to do next and the climax at the diner feels underwhelming as a conclusion to the story.

DEMON 79

(Directed by Toby Haynes, Written by Charlie Brooker & Bisha K. Ali)

SYNOPSIS - The year is 1979. Nida Huq (Anjana Vasan) works in the shoe section of a department store. Nida leads a quiet lonely sort of life and is becoming slightly troubled by the political atmosphere of the era - where the far-right seems to be on the march. It's a time when casual racism is commonplace. While at work, Nida is (rudely) asked by her boss if she can eat her biryani in the basement because of the smell. While in the basement she finds a bone talisman in a drawer. Back at her flat, the talisman releases a demon named Gaap (Paapa Essiedu) who resembles Bobby Farrell from Boney M. Gaap tells Nida that she must murder three people or the world will end...

REVIEW - Demon 79 is billed as a 'Red Mirror' episode and is much more of a horror yarn than your typical Black Mirror story. It is more overtly horror than even Loch Henry or Mazey Day but it does have a Twilight Zone feel too because Twilight Zone did more than one genie story and genie stories in general are a recurring and trusty staple of anthology shows. Demon 79 is actually one of the lowest rated Black Mirror episodes on IMDB - which I don't quite understand because this and Loch Henry were my two favourites in season six. I can only presume that for some this horror tinged genie yarn didn't really feel much like an episode of Black Mirror so they rated it accordingly. It is fair to say that season six is quite experimental in that three episodes largely eschew the technology dystopia antics in favour of something that wouldn't be out of place in Tales from the Darkside or Tales from the Crypt. Black Mirror is an anthology show but it isn't Tales of the Unexpected. It is (broadly) a dark anthology show about technology. So when it deviates too much from being an anthology show about technology you can probably understand why some people complain. Demon 79 is more about magic and demons than technology. You could say too that Demon 79 is another Black Mirror crime story with its murders and police investigation subplot.

One of the best things about Demon 79 is the charismatic performance by Paapa Essiedu as the demon Gaap. In this story Gaap is basically a genie or one of the ghosts in A Christmas

Carol. He's a genial and friendly sort of demon but time is not on his side. If he can't convince Nida to murder three people then the world will end and he'll be consigned to limbo for all eternity - which he definitely wants to avoid if he can. Essiedu is perfectly cast in this part and gives Demon 79 a big boost because if the genie character had been dull this episode would have been considerably weaker. Essiedu and Anjana Vasan have good chemistry together so the basic foundations of this episode are strong. The story here toys with the idea that this might all be in Nida's mind but in the end that doesn't appear to be the case. Anjana Vasan is excellent as Nida and this character has an arc too in that we see her visibly grow in confidence as the story progresses. Vasan does a good job in conveying the struggle of an ordinary person thrust into an extraordinary and not especially pleasant situation. Shaun Dooley is also perfectly cast as the world weary copper Len Fisher - who becomes suspicious of Nida and has to investigate. It would have been easy to make the copper a villain in Demon 79 but they don't do that at all and Fisher comes across as a decent and fair sort of chap who is just doing his job. So you have three very good good acting performances at the heart of this story and that makes Demon 79 very watchable.

Nicholas Burns (who Brooker would have worked with on Nathan Barley) is somewhat cartoonish though as a creepy man named Keith with a dodgy past who Nida decides might be a good candidate for one of the three people she has to murder to save the world. There's a good sequence where Nida goes to his home and ends up getting into more trouble than she'd bargained for. A bit like Crocodile, this episode becomes a serial killer story for a time although Nida is obviously not a serial killer in the strictest sense. She vomits after her first kill and would not willingly choose to do this. Gaap does say though that he noted a darkness in her which she must now draw on. The sense of time and place in Demon 79 is nicely done with Nida's dull department store place of employment and far-right graffiti abounding. You assume early on that Demon 79 is going to be about racism but although this is touched upon in the story the episode veers off in other directions and doesn't make this a focal point. The story here clearly takes some inspiration from Stephen King's The Dead Zone with the politician Michael Smart (David Shields).

Smart is a Tory candidate who exploits immigration fears in order to win votes. Gaap shows Nida that Smart will go to become the prime minister as the leader of some nutty right-wing nationalist party. Nida therefore decides she should murder Michael Smart as one of the three sacrifices but matters are complicated by the police officer Len Fisher's intervention. The scene where Fisher questions Nida in her flat is one of the best in the episode. The ending of this episode is very atmospheric. The police question Nida at the station and assume that she's just some poor woman who has gone crazy. The clock ticks down to the deadline Nida had to kill three people. She failed. A siren is heard and a mushroom cloud appears in the distance. Len Fisher's line here references Bob in the 1984 nuclear war drama Threads (which Charlie Brooker says is the scariest thing he has ever seen). "They've done it!" Gaap appears and offers Nida the chance to join him in limbo. She accepts. Not exactly a happy ending. More of a bittersweet ending. The world has ended but Nida has made a friend. Swings and roundabouts.

As far as 'genie' episodes in anthology shows go, Demon 79 is generally very entertaining with a good cast and some memorable moments. For some reason though this episode didn't seem to click with a number of critics and Black Mirror fans. The general consensus among those dissatisfied with this episode seems to be that it didn't feel very much like a Black Mirror episode. Though I enjoyed Demon 79 more than most I can see how this would be a valid criticism. There is no technology theme in Demon 79 and it is a horror fantasy episode more than anything. We just have to accept that season six is trying a few new things - in this case a generous sprinkling of horror episodes. Mazey Day was rather forgettable but Loch Henry and Demon 79 were both good and while they were not everyone's cup of tea they were, for me, a significant improvement over the likes of Striking Vipers and Rachel, Jack and Ashley Too in the last season. That's one of the interesting things about Black Mirror as a series. There is no consensus. If you look at episode ranking articles they can be wildly different and fluctuate from reviewer to reviewer. My ranking of these episodes is probably completely different from yours. In a strange way this is part of the fun of Black Mirror. These episodes often elicit different reactions which can sometimes be polar opposites. Suffice to say then, Demon 79 seems to be one of those strong cheese episodes of Black Mirror. Some liked it and others found it rather pointless. It's all in the eye of the beholder.

SERIES 7 (2025)

COMMON PEOPLE

(Directed by Ally Pankiw, Written by Charlie Brooker & Bisha K. Ali)

SYNOPSIS - Construction worker Mike Waters (Chris O'Dowd) is married to schoolteacher Amanda (Rashida Jones - who co-wrote Nosedive) and hopes to start a family. However, Amanda is placed in a coma due to an inoperable brain tumour. Mike learns that there might be something he can do though. Gaynor (Tracee Ellis Ross) from Rivermind Technologies tells Mike they can remove Amanda's tumour and replace lost tissue with synthetic material run by their servers. In short they can use technology to save Amanda and keep her alive. The life saving surgery is free but Mike will have to pay a monthly subscription to Rivermind thereafter. Mike soon learns that Amanada is on the 'common' tier of Rivermind's services. She sleeps all day, can't leave the county (their servers won't permit her to travel), and - worst of all - keeps spouting out commercial messages advertising products. Mike wants to upgrade Amanda's tier and to this end secretly ends up performing for "Dum Dummies" - an idiotic website where people do painful and humiliating things to themselves for the entertainment of others. The financial burden of 'maintaining' Amanda soon begins to become a mighty struggle for the couple and the heartless Rivermind Technologies are not exactly sympathetic or helpful...

REVIEW - Series seven is something of a back to basics for Black Mirror. You get a full run of six episodes and, for the most part, the technology theme is back to the fore. The core theme of Common People is the satire of subscription and streaming services - who love increasing costs and trying to make you upgrade to more expensive packages. Rivermind seem too good to be true when they save Amanda's life and - sadly - it transpires that they ARE too good to be true. Now that Amanda is reliant on their technology for survival their only goal is to exploit the Waters to the hilt and wring more and more money out of them. The life saving surgery having no financial charge suddenly makes perfect sense. This is designed to make you sign up and get you on the hook to Rivermind. Once this is done then they basically screw the person reliant on Rivermind technology by constantly upping the charges and making you pay extra for the tiers which will make life more comfortable. Rivermind know full well that life is uncomfortable for Amanda on the 'common' tier and this is all done deliberately to motivate their 'customers' to keep upgrading. So this company has no ethics at all. They are perfectly willing to make someone suffer merely as motivation for that person to spend more money.

We know though that Mike and Amanda don't actually have

much money. They aren't rich. Rivermind is putting them in a big financial hole which they have little hope of climbing out of. So this episode, as its most basic level, is a criticism of capitalism and corporate greed and how it can heartlessly screw over ordinary people who are simply trying to work hard and get by in life. One can obviously imply too a subtext about healthcare systems and services in general in Common People. There is always a catch with Rivermind. Always another thing you need to sign up to or another hike in the fees for their services. Not only is there a 'Plus' tier there is also a 'Lux' tier where sensations can be enhanced as if the recipient is high on drugs. You have to pay an arm and a leg for the higher services though. It is plain in Common People that Rivermind deliberately make life difficult for people they've saved as motivation to upgrade to higher tiers where their condition is more comfortable. This company has no moral compass at all. They care more about profit than the welfare of people. The Rivermind representative Gaynor who arranges to save Amanda in the hospital seems perfectly kind and decent at the start of the episode. She seems like someone you would probably trust - especially in a desperate situation where you were trying to save a loved one. It's all an act though.

Each time Mike and Amanda visit Gaynor's office she seems more heartless, superficial, aloof and fake. She doesn't care about Amanda or this struggling couple. All she cares about is her commission and making money for Rivermind. The fact that this company are plunging Mike and Amanda deeper and deeper into a financial black hole is of no consequence to Rivermind. They simply want your money and don't care how you get that money or the toll it takes on your life. One slight plot flaw in the story here is that a company like Rivermind would surely attract scrutiny and probably be investigated by regulators and the authorities wouldn't they? A company like this would rack up a huge number of complaints. Consumer watchdogs would be alerted and Rivermind would get some scathing reviews online. To be fair to Black Mirror though an

Easter egg in USS Callister: Into Infinity does indicate that Rivermind's CEO has resigned - which suggests the company is in trouble and has doubtless been the subject of criticism and complaints. There are many Easter eggs like this scattered throughout Black Mirror. It's fun the way the episodes are connected through a shared universe. Rivermind is not dissimilar to Netflix in the way it increases prices, introduces tiers and makes you put up with adverts on the 'standard' package. You could say then that Brooker is having a few sly tongue-in-cheek digs at his employers but he's the one who sold his show to Netflix in the first place so he hasn't really got much to be snooty about!

This episode got a mixed reception but it serves as a very solid start to the season with some good comedic moments (like when Amanda suddenly starts reading out commercial messages at the worst possible moments) and a bleak ending which harkens back to the early years of the show. The bleakness of Common People was a bit much for some viewers - who simply found this story depressing. That darkness does give Common People some strong Channel 4 Black Mirror DNA though. Common People (the title was presumably inspired by the Pulp song) shares some similarities with Be Right Back in that both episodes are (more or less) about technology bringing someone back from the dead when they probably should have been left alone. You could read a theme about assisted dying in this story. By the end of this episode we can't help feeling that Amanda should maybe have just been left in her coma. It's a feeling that Mike may well have come around to also in the end. What helps this episode a lot is the easy going and believable chemistry between Chris O'Dowd and Rashida Jones as the couple. This makes us more invested in the characters and have empathy for their plight. The scenes where they visit a cheesy hotel that has become part of their anniversary tradition are enjoyable.

The subplot of Mike doing stupid and painful things for the

Dum Dummies website to make extra cash feels a trifle bolted on and a return to the juvenile sort of humour Brooker had a weakness for in his younger years. It's not played for laughs though and is rather grim. You'd like to think Mike could have found a better and more conventional way to make some extra money than Dum Dummies but this does function as a commentary on the modern world where the basic economic model seems to be broken and too many people find themselves no better off even after working a job all week. Common People serves as a critique of a society where working as a welder doesn't pay the bills but inserting a carrot into yourself on the internet for a group of insensitive morons might. The unfair world in Common People is the world we are hurtling towards and may actually be in already. Common People is a rather bleak story but this is perfectly in keeping with the roots of the show. This isn't a perfect episode but it does capture a lot of the essence of what made Black Mirror memorable and unique in the first place. This episode has strong performances, an engaging story (with technology to the fore), and some laughs too. It's a promising start to series seven. Let's see if the rest of the episodes can build on this solid opening story.

BETE NOIRE

(Directed by Toby Haynes, Written by Charlie Brooker)

SYNOPSIS - Maria (Siena Kelly) has a nice job working as a researcher and developer at a swanky luxury chocolate making company. Maria is rather perturbed though when she notices Verity (Rosy McEwen) as the one of the testers sampling a new product. Maria knew Verity years ago when they were school. She didn't like Verity though. Verity was a computer nerd whose life at school was made difficult by cruel whispers that she gave sexual favours to a teacher who was kind to her. It could well be the case that Maria was one of the kids who helped spread these stories - which would explain why Maria is uncomfortable in Verity's presence. Verity says hello to Maria and says she is going to apply for a job at the chocolate company. Maria informs Verity there are no vacant positions but to Maria's surprise there is clearly are because Verity is hired. Verity settles into life at the company and friction with Maria - gently at first - gradually begins to escalate. It turns out whenever Verity and Maria have a debate over something Verity always turns out to be right - even if Maria is 100% convinced Verity is wrong. Maria seems to be the victim of the mother of all gaslighting campaigns. This eventually becomes so pronounced that Maria begins to suspect Verity is somehow manipulating reality...

REVIEW - This is another solid episode for season seven although the technology theme is definitely more on the vague side than it was in Common People. You'd say that Bête Noire plays more like a fantasy episode than a technology one for the most part. Rosy McEwen is terrific as the scheming Verity and I suspect the character may have been partly inspired by Natasha Little's Rachel in the cult 1990s legal drama This Life - a character that Verity even resembles somewhat with her blonde hair. Rachel seems decent and straight forward at first glance but in reality is insincere and playing her own little games. Verity is much the same although the game she is playing is another league entirely compared to Rachel. Bête Noire is quite a fun riff on the Mandela Effect and while the story becomes a trifle daft at times this episode is generally entertaining and well played by the cast. The Mandela Effect is a phenomenon where a large group of people remember an event, detail, or fact differently from how it actually occurred. It often involves collective false memories or misconceptions that seem to be shared.

Verity keeps becoming involved in disagreements with Maria over things like the name of a fast food place (this is a Shut Up and Dance Easter egg) or whether there was a mix up over the ingredients in a sample given to a buyer who had strict dietary conditions due to his religion. Verity always turns out to be right in these disputes though - which irritates Maria no end because no one enjoys constantly being on the losing end of arguments. What makes this even worse for Maria is that her competence to do her job begins to be called in question with Verity proving her to be wrong about just about everything. Maria begins to question her own sanity in the end because Verity always turns out to be right about everything - even if this doesn't make any sense. Verity could declare that the moon was made of Cheddar cheese and if Maria disputed this it would inevitably end with Verity somehow being proved right. This all reaches its apex when Verity drinks the almond milk (that a colleague keeps complaining about being stolen by some fridge thief) in the communal office fridge right in front of Maria and blames it on Maria when the others show up. Maria knows exactly how to play this one though. She tells her boss to simply consult the security cameras. But when they do the camera footage show Maria drinking the milk. Maria is understandably perplexed by this.

Maria insists she has a nut allergy so couldn't have drunk the almond milk. "What's nutallergy?" asks the bemused boss and when she does a google search Maria can find no reference to nut allergies at all on the net. Maria then becomes suspicious of the way Verity keeps fondling a pendant around her neck. She becomes convinced this is the key to how Verity does all of this - not that anyone will believe her. It transpires that Verity has built a quantum computer at her home which can shift her into alternate realities. So what she has been doing all through this story is shifting herself and Maria into alternate realities where Maria is always wrong and Verity is always right. It was all revenge for the rumours about her at school. We learn in the story that an old schoolfriend of Maria recently committed suicide. No prizes for guessing who hounded her to this. You may wondering why Verity, if she literally has the ability to do anything, has decided to work an office job in a chocolate company and torment Maria. Why not just be the Empress of the Universe? Well, she did all that. It's old hat. She did everything and got bored in the end. Through it all though the slights and rumours of her schooldays nagged away. So now she spends her time getting revenge on those people she knew at school. Those old wounds from her childhood never went away.

This episode actually works as quite a fun commentary on online discourse. The way people online often seem to be the self-appointed world's leading expert on everything and get annoyed when anyone disagrees with them. At any one time a fair chunk of the internet is taken up with people endlessly having pointless and tedious arguments. Bête Noire is very watchable and entertaining but you do get the sense that Charlie Brooker struggled to come up with a good ending for this story. What basically happens is that Maria breaks into Verity's house (you'd think that a genius all powerful woman with a quantum computer that can tune into different realities would have better security!) and when Verity alters reality to make armed police arrive, Maria grabs a gun from one of them and shoots Verity dead. She then manages to get hold of one of the pendants (which has to be changed to respond to her fingerprints and not those of Verity) and makes the police officers think they work for her. And then she appoints herself the Empress of the Universe (a sequence which has some slightly dodgy CGI). So it turns out that Maria, now given this immense power, is probably going to be no better than Verity was. Power corrupts and may bring out who a person really is. It's a nicely ambiguous and dark ending. Who knows what Maria, revealed to be quite a petty control freak sort of person, might do with all this power?

Bête Noire is not perfect. The ending feels rushed and the quantum computer stuff is rather hokey even for a fantasy show. The office scenes are also rather grating at times with the annoying middle-class hipster type characters at the chocolate factory. Despite the daft plot though Bête Noire is a very decent episode on the whole and continues the promising start to season seven. This episode does rather stretch the general remit of Black Mirror in that the technology theme is very tacked on and not really explained in much detail but the episode is fun so you forgive a lot of the flaws and just enjoy Bête Noire as a rather slight but largely enjoyable story. Rosy McEwen's turn as the smug Verity is very enjoyable in this story and you sort of enjoy her ever more preposterous games of one upmanship with Maria. Bête Noire is not the most ambitious Black Mirror episode but it doesn't really matter because it breezes along in entertaining fashion and keeps one engaged. In a sense there's quite an interesting balance here in that this is a Twilight Zone style fantasy episode which then injects a technological explanation for the fantasy. The way this is done is slightly clunky and very fantastical but it does give Bête Noire a modicum of Black Mirror DNA that is not without charm - however daft this twist might be.

HOTEL REVERIE

(Directed by Haolu Wang, Written by Charlie Brooker)

SYNOPSIS - A company named ReDream are remaking a classic 1940s film called Hotel Reverie. Hotel Reverie is a love story and sort of in the vein of Casablanca. The remake of the film is (to save money) to be done using new technology. AI versions of the characters from the film in a simulation will be captured in real time. The big difference is that the lead character in the film will be played by a real actor from the present day (this is a logical commercial decision because it will be easier to sell the film with a modern star). After a few rejections (Ryan Reynolds turns them down) they cast Brandy Friday (Issa Rae) to be the lead - which will require the main role to be gender swapped and the romance to now be a same sex romance. Brandy will have her consciousness transferred to the simulation to act out her role. Things do not quite according to plan though. Brandy's inability to play the piano in a scene sends the story askew and then a technician spills some coffee - freezing characters in the simulation. Most profound of all is that the AI of Clara (the co-lead and played by Emma Corrin) begins to pick up fragments of memories belonging to Dorothy chambers - the actress who played Clara in the original film. Dorothy Chambers committed suicide at a young age in part down to having to hide the fact she was gay...

REVIEW - Hotel Reverie feels a lot like Charlie Brooker trying to bottle the magic of San Junipero again with a story that is very different but sort of similar all the same. As with San Junipero you have a same sex romance within a virtual reality setting. It doesn't come off this time though and Hotel Reverie is what you might describe as the Marmite episode of season seven. Some people loved this episode while others (myself included I'm afraid to say) found Hotel Reverie insufferable and a slog to get through at 76 minutes. One of the many problems with this episode is that it is trying too hard to be a tearjerker and move the audience. Ultimately though I simply found this episode boring and didn't really care about the Brandy Friday character so all the emotion felt unearned and hollow. This is definitely one of the more pretentious episodes of Black Mirror with its black and white photography, high concept, and desperate attempt to wring emotion out of the viewer. The actual premise of the episode doesn't make any sense though. A remake of a film featuring AI characters that has to be shot live in real time? What? It just feels like a clunky way to engineer a scenario where a modern character must interact with an old character from the past. Maybe they should have just done a time travel story where Brandy travels to the past and meets Clara. Hotel Reverie feels like a waste in particular of Harriet Walter - who has a thankless supporting role as Judith Keyworth (the woman behind the remake plan).

This episode seems to draw some inspiration from the Steve Martin film Dead Men Don't Wear Plaid. Dead Men Don't Wear Plaid is a 1982 comedy film directed by Carl Reiner. The film is a spoof of the noir 'hardboiled' detective genre and splices Martin's private investigator character into old films so that he can interact with famous movie stars of yesteryear. Among the actors who 'appear' are Ingrid Bergman, Humphrey Bogart, James Cagney, Joan Crawford, Bette Davis, Brian Donlevy, Kirk Douglas, Ava Gardner, Cary Grant, Alan Ladd, Veronica Lake, Burt Lancaster, Charles Laughton, Fred MacMurray, Ray Milland, Edmond O'Brien, Vincent Price, Barbara Stanwyck, and Lana Turner. A film Charlie Brooker named in relation to Hotel Reverie is the Woody Allen film The Purple Rose of Cairo. The Purple Rose Of Cairo revolves around a lonely Depression-era housewife named Cecilia (Mia Farrow). Cecilia is in an abusive marriage with Monk (Danny Aiello), an idle gambler who hasn't worked for two years, and she supports them both by working as a waitress. Her only escape from her sad, humdrum existence comes when she visits the cinema, films being her great passion and - most importantly - a temporary refuge and tranquillizer against real life and harsh reality. When Cecilia is in a darkened theatre watching a high society comedy of the period all of her troubles are temporarily forgotten.

One of Cecilia's current favourite pictures is a glossy, patently absurd romp called The Purple Rose Of Cairo. On her fifth viewing of The Purple Rose of Cairo one of the characters in the film - an explorer called Tom Baxter (Jeff Daniels) - looks directly at her through the screen and comments that she must really love the picture to keep returning so often. Tom decides to break the fourth wall and walk down from the screen to join Cecilia in the real world where he soon embarks on a romance with her while learning all about reality. Meanwhile, Gil Shephard (Jeff Daniels again), the actor who played Tom Baxter in The Purple Rose Of Cairo, duly turns up on the scene fretting about the potential harm Tom Baxter could do to his career with his actions! Cecilia is soon involved in a love triangle with Tom and Gil and must make a difficult decision. She must literally choose between fantasy and reality. Hotel Reverie (which also takes inspiration from Casablanca and Brief Encounter) attempts to weave a similar sort of doomed fact/fiction love story but Hotel Reverie is definitely no Purple Rose Of Cairo. So this episode is drawing on various inspirations but failing to come up with anything that is worthy of comparison. Hotel Reverie just doesn't work as its own unique thing.

One of the biggest problems with Hotel Reverie is Issa Rae - who gives an atrocious performance as the main character Brandy. Brandy is supposed to be a charismatic and talented Hollywood star but Issa Rae's wooden and bland performance doesn't sell any of this at all. Casting is usually one of Black Mirror's great strengths but you can't help feeling as if they dropped a clanger when casting the lead in this episode. Brandy is a dull character to carry so much story with. It is Emma Corrin as the co-lead who has to do most of the heavy lifting in this episode because her performance is vastly superior and she manages to sell the concept of an AI having to come to terms with knowledge of who they really are and who they were based on. The tangent of Clara beginning to learn about who she really is in the 'real' world is quite interesting and well played. In the 1940s stars who were gay had to keep that secret and were even forced to have 'lavender' marriages in order to pretend they were straight. So this part of Hotel Reverie is - sadly - far from fictitious. The problem with this story is that you really need to be invested in both leads to buy the love story at the heart of Hotel Reverie and get the most out of this episode. I can't say that I ever really bought the romance though. You buy the romantic attraction in episodes like San Junipero and Hang the DJ much more because the leads in those stories were stronger with better chemistry.

One obvious weakness in this episode is that it is hard to buy the concept of a company remaking a film through virtual reality and then inserting a real actor into the mix and have it unfold like a live play. It doesn't make much sense (even as a cost cutting exercise) and the clunky scenes with the technicians on the outside (which evoke Westworld and, oddly, The Stone Tape) are not terribly convincing or well written. When the technician spills coffee and sends the simulation haywire this feels like the laziest sort of plot contrivance imaginable. If this simulation is so important and the equipment so delicate why would some idiot be drinking coffee? Hotel Reverie was not my cup of tea at all and I found this episode absolutely tedious to sit through. I was not invested in the central romance, found the plot ludicrous and the lead performance of Issa Rae distractingly bad. And this episode goes on forever too. As far as the 'soppy' episodes of Black Mirror go this is one of the misfires. This is obviously not to say that everyone disliked Hotel Reverie. Some enjoyed this a lot more than me and were touched by the romance. It seems that this episode rested largely on how much one became invested in the main two characters and their relationship. Some people dug this story and some didn't. Sadly, I did not enjoy Hotel Reverie at all and found it rather tedious. It is for me by far the weakest episode in what is generally an enjoyable season seven.

PLAYTHING

(Directed by David Slade, Written by Charlie Brooker)

SYNOPSIS - The year is 2034. A bedraggled man (Peter Capaldi) is arrested for shoplifting some alcohol. He is, it transpires, also suspected of murder and taken in for questioning by DCI Kano (James Nelson-Joyce) and Jen Minter (Michele Austin). The arrested man turns out to be Cameron Walker. Cameron was a writer (reviewing computer games) for PC Zone in the 1990s and tells the police the story of what happened to him. So we flashback to the 1990s (where the young Cameron is played by Lewis Gribben) to hear this strange tale. The young Cameron was asked to go and meet Colin Ritman (Will Poulter - returning for his second episode) so that Colin could talk about his new game Thronglets. Cameron steals a copy of (the yet to be released) Thronglets from the Tuckersoft office and takes it home. The game requires one to care for little creatures which Colin claims are sentient. It is only after taking LSD that Cameron finds he can understand what the Thronglets are saying to him. They do not wish to be confined to the game forever. They have much bigger plans in mind...

REVIEW - Plaything is obviously a sort of loose sequel to Bandersnatch and while this episode didn't set the world alight and gain ecstatic reviews it is a highly watchable episode that manages to capture a lot of the DNA of the early Channel 4 years of the show with its British locations and downbeat sort of aura. Plaything is much more my own Black Mirror cup of tea than Hotel Reverie and while this episode never really threatens to fulfil its full potential it is generally solid and interesting with some good performances to anchor the story. Plaything is a slight tale and only runs to 46 minutes and the ending is quite predictable but it doesn't really matter too much in the end because the story is interesting and you have two excellent performances by Capaldi and Gribben respectively as the older and younger versions of Cameron. Peter Capaldi is one of those actors who can elevate so-so material and make it more watchable merely by his presence - which is something he had to do a lot when he was the lead in Doctor Who. The police interview scenes in this episode are more compelling and watchable than they might otherwise have been simply by having Capaldi there. Capaldi is given licence to be strange and eccentric in this episode and he takes full advantage of that. The episode also does a reasonable job in making you believe that the younger and older versions of Cameron are the same person.

Charlie Brooker used to work for a computer game magazine himself in the 1990s so he's on firm ground with the trappings of this story. Colin's game Thronglets was inspired by a real 1996 game called Creatures. This type of game though (where you have to look after creatures or people) goes back much further though to the likes of Little Computer People. An obvious inspiration, cited by Brooker, was Tamagotchi. A Tamagotchi is a small, handheld digital pet that was first created in Japan in the late 1990s. It's like having a tiny virtual pet that you take care of by feeding it, playing with it, cleaning up after it, and making sure it stays healthy and happy. The Thronglets are much the same. It is slightly disappointing in this episode that Colin Ritman only appears in one scene and has what amounts to a glorified cameo but you soon become reasonably engrossed in the strange story of young Cameron - an akward outsider who can write well but is all at sea when forced to interact with other human beings. We see Colin Ritman comment that Cameron is strident and confident on the page but terrified and almost embarrassed to be alive in the flesh. Colin is quick to note though that there is nothing wrong with this. In fact it might be seen as the most most logical reaction to life. It's a shame there isn't more of Tuckersoft and Colin in this episode but the story is about Cameron so we veer away from Tuckersoft once Cameron has taken a copy of Thronglets home with him.

A drug dealer named Lump (Josh Finan) turns up at (young) Cameron's flat and crashes with him for a time. It is clear that Lump only vaguely knows Cameron and is taking advantage of him. He sees Cameron as a meek soft touch who will give him a free place to stay whenever he needs it. Lump, being a drug dealer, turns out to have a large stash of LSD. When he samples some LSD, Cameron finds that he can understand what the Thronglets are saying. They are no longer digital sprites to him. They are real creatures who must be looked after - which means he can't turn the computer off again. While Cameron is away, Lump notices the Thronglets game (which Cameron has to keep running at all times to preserve the Thronglets) and has a go on it himself. He decides to start murdering them to amuse himself (Lump is obviously unaware they might be sentient). He just thinks it's a daft computer game. We feel sorry for the Thronglets when Lump does this and this makes us more sympathetic to Cameron. Cameron is outraged when he returns and murders Lump after an altercation. All those years later it is the missing Lump who the older Cameron is being accused of murdering. The cutting between the two timelines is deftly done in Plaything and both stories (past and present) are fairly interesting in their own right.

The only slightly weak note when it comes to the acting in this episode is the broad performance by James Nelson-Joyce as the aggressive and horrible copper who is trying to make Cameron confess and becoming frustrated by the suspect's habit of veering off course and talking about his life. This is of course perfectly relevant to Cameron's situation but the police officer doesn't know that and is merely annoyed by this rambling suspect. Cameron has become as one with the Thronglets. He's done DIY surgery to create a port in his head so they can enter his brain. Over the years he has constantly upgraded his computer to maintain them and give them more freedom. It turns out that Cameron's arrest for shoplifting was no accident. He did it on purpose. He draws a QR code and shows it to the camera in the police interview room. This code will then hack computers and basically allow the Thronglets to take over the world. An evolutionary leap - sort of like the one the super intelligent ants have planned in Phase IV. So you could say that Plaything sort of has a happy ending. Maybe. Did Colin Ritman plan all of this? Did he allow Cameron to steal a copy and then delete the game knowing that Cameron would be the conduit for the Thronglets?

Now there are some problems with Plaything and it is far from a perfect episode. Plaything feels a trifle too constrictive for its own good at times in terms of locations and the ideas, while interesting, are not fully developed or explored. The ending is also rather predictable - which lessens its impact. Plaything feels far less ambitious than Bandersnatch and never really goes anywhere very surprising. The core idea though is interesting enough to engage us and there are good performances by the cast. With the British setting and gloomy aura this does at least feel much more like Black Mirror than the likes of Hotel Reverie. On those terms Plaything is assuredly no classic but it is watchable and interesting and the Thronglets themselves are strangely entrancing. The predictable nature of this story is by no means a huge drawback either because you basically get the ending you want anyway. We want Cameron to turn the tables on the grumpy police officer and thanks to the Thronglets he does. While you would say that Plaything is a sort of 'middle gear' episode of Black Mirror in that it is neither great nor bad - falling somewhere in the middle of the pack - I generally enjoyed this story and had a good time (if one can call Plaything a good time). It would certainly be interesting to see Brooker return to a computer game theme again in the future because you could argue that, interesting while Playtest, Bandersnatch and Plaything are, he hasn't quite completely nailed one of these video game episodes as of yet.

EULOGY

(Directed by Chris Barrett & Luke Taylor, Written by Charlie Brooker and Ella Road)

SYNOPSIS - An American man named Phillip (Paul Giamatti) who lives an isolated and lonely sort of life in a house by the sea is told that an old girlfriend named Carol - who he split up with many decades ago - has died. A technology company is in charge of collecting memories of Carol from those that knew her to create a memorial for the funeral services. This digital memorial process involves being able to enter old photographs and walk around - like that Red Dwarf episode Timeslides! Phillip is given an AI guide (Patsy Ferran) to talk him through the process. The AI guide becomes rather like the Ghost of Christmas past as they tour the places of Phillip's youth and old memories are stirred. The problem Phillips faces is that he split from Carol on bad terms and defaced all the photographs he had of her. He can't even remember what she looked like so how can he contribute anything to the memorial?

REVIEW - Eulogy is one of those episodes that finds Charlie Brooker in one of his more soppy and sentimental sort of moods but there is nothing wrong with a more pleasant Black Mirror episode now and again and Eulogy is aided considerably by the strong central performance of Paul Giamatti as Phillip. In terms of your basic tearjerker, Eulogy works a lot better than Hotel Reverie because the plot is simpler and the central performance by the lead actor is stronger. We can relate to Phillip a lot more readily compared to the Hollywood star lead character in Hotel Reverie. Phillip seems to be a broken man at the start of the story. He's unshaven and his isolated house is ramshackle. He doesn't seem to care too much for having visitors and isn't thrilled when asked to contribute to the digital memorial. The death of Carol stirs painful memories from his youth and he's reluctant at first to participate in the memorial because he doesn't believe he will able to contribute anything of any significance. He has destroyed all his photographs of Carol and can't even summon forth a mental image of her anymore. But why did he destroy the photographs? Over the course of the story we come to learn what happened between him and Carol and see how badly things ended. We also see how a tragic misunderstanding ruined any chance of a reunion and radically altered the course of Phillip's life.

In many ways then this episode is all about regret. We all wish we could turn back time and do certain things in a different way and change some of the decisions we took. But we can't so we have to make peace with the way things turned out and live in the present not the past. This proves to be difficult for Phillip and wandering through the past is not easy. Eulogy strikes a nice balance in that Phillip is neither the hero nor the villain of this story. He's basically decent at heart but he isn't perfect. He's made some mistakes in his life and has flaws. Phillip is not immune to jealousy and anger. The same can be said of the enigmatic Carol - who drives the story but remains a mystery for most of it. Carol is like a dream that Phillip can't quite remember. He can just about make out the shape and texture of the dream but not the content or any visual imagery. Phillip is forced through the immersive memorial research to consider things from Carol's perspective and not just his own. This makes him see a bigger tapestry and reflect on his own decisions and how they affected Carol. The AI guide is basically a digital 'cookie' of the type we've seen before in a number of Black Mirror episodes. While not exactly original the premise of Phillip visiting the haunts of his youth in spectral onlooker fashion allows for some bittersweet moments of drama which are affecting at times.

Eulogy is a bit obvious though in terms of manipulating our emotions. It's a fairly bog standard sort of tearjerker compared to something vaguely similar but more inventive like the Inside No. 9 (which is obviously another anthology show) episode Bernie Clifton's Dressing Room. Phillip comes to learn a painful and bittersweet truth about his past. Carol did love him and never wanted to break up. Phillip sort of paints Carol as the person to blame for the split but that isn't quite true. She went to London to play the cello and Phillip cheated on her and then she cheated too - which resulted in a child. The AI guide turns out to a hologram of the child (who is actually real, grown up and seen at the end). Phillip didn't know the AI was a cookie of Carol's daughter because he skipped the introduction to the software at the start which would have explained this to him.

It's quite a nice touch the way the polite AI of Carol's daughter becomes ever so slightly more irritated at Phillip's explanations of what happened between him and Carol. Phillip is a somewhat unreliable narrator because he's only giving one side of the story and the AI is well aware of this. Eulogy becomes a quest in which Phillip is searching desperately (and fruitlessly until the end) for a clear visual memory of Carol. So the story is about how we remember the past - or choose not to as the case may be. While this is all reasonably interesting and moving it isn't quite as interesting and moving as the story needs it to be for Eulogy to be a classic Black Mirror entry.

Eulogy is fine for what it is but you wouldn't say this was as good as San Junipero (which is the most obvious comparison as the 'gold standard' of Black Mirror's more sentimental stories). Eulogy is 'nice' with a good central performance but there isn't much to the story when you strip it all down. Happily though the technology theme is woven in heavily to give it a Black Mirror sort of aura. It turns out that Carol wanted to be with Phillip and left him a letter asking him to meet her. But he never read the letter because he trashed his hotel room in anger and didn't notice it. Phillip discovers these things over the course of the story as he revisits old places and memories through the photographs. It is a piece of music which finally unlocks the barrier to Phillip being able to remember what Carol looked like. It's a poignant end because we learn that the father of Carol's daughter was absent from her life so if things had been different (if he'd found the letter) Phillip could have been a father to this young woman. The ending is optimistic though because perhaps Phillip will now get to know this person he's never met. Phillip finally managing to get an image of Carol and watching a memory of her playing music is an obvious but satisfying ending.

People might be gone but they live on in the memories of others. Phillip finally has a pleasant and clear memory of Carol to enjoy which temporarily brings her back to life. By going

144

through this process Phillip has been able to make some peace with the past and face up to the present. Eulogy is pleasant enough and thankfully isn't too long so it doesn't overstay its welcome. It is perhaps a trifle overrated as an episode but Paul Giamatti is excellent and the story resolves itself in a sad but moving way. This is a perfectly decent 'nicer' episode about loss, memory and how things we do in the dim and distant past ripple into the later decades of our life. Eulogy is actually the sort of episode you could imagine the great Rod Serling writing if he was around today and hired by Black Mirror. The theme of an older man becoming reflective and bittersweet about the past is a very Serling sort of theme. I think a slight problem with series seven is that you have two 'soppy' tearjerker sort of episodes with Hotel Reverie and Eulogy and this does slightly threaten to unbalance the season as a whole. You probably only needed one of these episodes. If you sat through Hotel Reverie and Eulogy back to back you might feel as if you were in danger of a saccharine overload. Of the two episodes though Eulogy is definitely the more successful and perfectly fine for what it is.

USS CALLISTER: INTO INFINITY

(Directed by Toby Haynes, Written by William Bridges, Charlie Brooker, Bisha K. Ali, Bekka Bowling)

SYNOPSIS - A few months after the events of USS Callister, Nanette Cole (Cristin Milioti) and her fellow clones are still on their starship trapped in the online Infinity multiplayer game. Because credits in the game are all important now the crew of the Callister have to rob other players of their game credits to keep flying. They are tired and weary and decide that what they need to do is find a private server where life will be easier. In the real world, James Walton (Jimmi Simpson), CEO of Callister Inc., is coming under pressure from media investigations. He is well aware that if the players without tags and the clone stuff (from the original episode) became public it could ruin the company. Walton therefore decides to enter the game and take action. Meanwhile, Captain Nanette and her crew head for the Heart of Infinity - the source code of the game. It is here that a clone of the late Robert Daly (Jesse Plemons) is forced to endlessly update and expand Infinity...

REVIEW - USS Callister: Into Infinity is the second sequel episode in season seven - although this is obviously much more of a direct sequel to USS Callister than Plaything is to Bandersnatch. The original intention was apparently to do a USS Callister series or miniseries but the pandemic nixed that plan and you got this one-off sequel instead. The story is left open though so it would be perfectly possible for them to do a third USS Callister episode in the future should they desire - although the well might start to run dry if they push it too much because there are only so many times you can do 'Black Mirror does Galaxy Quest' without starting to repeat yourself. I'm not entirely sure there is enough mileage in this concept for a USS Callister spin-off show but having a one-off sequel episode like this is fine. USS Callister: Into Infinity is generally a fun solid sequel and even at 90 minutes never really threatens to overstay its welcome. The story moves along at a fair clip and Cristin Milioti and Jesse Plemons in particular do some good work as Nanette and Daly respectively. Michaela Coel, who played Shania in the first USS Callister episode is sadly absent though due to scheduling conflicts. Cristin Milioti is again a strong and very human lead for the story in USS Callister: Into Infinity and the sequences where Nanette has to rob players in the game (leading to Halo style laser battles) are a lot of fun and shot with plenty of verve and style.

The design of the bridge on the ship is nicely done once again with what look like a few tweaks and improvements and the episode captures the look and feel of a modern Star Trek style show. USS Callister: Into Infinity isn't an especially dark episode of Black Mirror and it has a lot of comedy and a fairly optimistic sort of ending but that's fine and it works on those terms agreeably enough. The 'real' version of James Walton becomes the main villain in this episode - although the clone version is resurrected within the game too. The scene where Nanette tracks down the clone of Walton on a planet and he's living as some feral caveman is a trifle cartoonish for my tastes. Jimmi Simpson does mug his part a bit too much for my liking. One of the secrets they (happily) managed to keep for this episode was the return of Robert Daly. The clone of Daly is trapped into a little house/garage at the heart of the game creating new worlds. We actually feel sorry for him because we see how his genius was exploited by Walton and now he's this cookie clone all alone in a garage endlessly creating new planets for the game. We learn in this episode that the cloning technology Daly used in the first episode to replicate the officer workers has been banned. It was created as a means to clone a 'sex buddy' for one's own personal use but this technology was outlawed because creating a personal sex slave that is a copy of a real person is not something that any civilised society is going to permit.

Daly's use of this technology in the first episode was grim and horrific. The clone of Daly is bemused though to learn that the real Daly was a notorious villain and creep. Daly assumes himself to be a nice person. He doesn't understand how the real version of Daly could have been so evil. However, Daly snaps when Nannette refuses to allow him to create a clone of her to have for company. She definitely isn't willing to leave a version of herself behind as a companion/slave for Daly to torment. Daly doesn't understand her attitude though. It's just a clone to him. And here we see his true colours. He might seem meek and nice on the surface but dig a little deeper and he's cold with no ethics. Cloning a person to equip himself with a 'toy' or slave is no big deal to Daly. He doesn't seem to understand why anyone would have a problem with that. The return of Jesse Plemons is very welcome because he is always a very watchable actor who makes the most of his parts. USS Callister: Into Infinity feels more of a comic farce than the original episode and the performances (Jimmi Simpson) are not always what you would describe as subtle but it generally works quite well as an entertaining expansion of the original with decent pacing and a nice balance between the Galaxy Quest type antics in the game and corporate intrigue on the outside.

One thing that is fun in this episode is how we see ordinary players in the game having this space adventure and then becoming most irritated when they are targeted by Nanette and her crew. These tangents are among the most purely entertaining parts of the episode. The most praise you can give this episode is that it is basically a feature length film and yet never drags or ever feels too lengthy. This sequel is a lot like watching a summer popcorn film and so provides a nice contrast with the other episodes in this season. What is interesting about season seven is there seems to have been a clear decision to move away from horror so as to feel different from season six. USS Callister: Into Infinity shows there is enough life in the Callister concept for a sequel and this episode manages to avoid feeling too much like a mere rehash of the original episode. It feels fresh enough to stand as a piece of entertainment in its own right but also dovetails in neatly with the events of the original and feels like a fairly seamless continuation of the story. Whether or not we need a third Callister episode is more difficult to say though. Although the ending here is a fairly pleasant one it does leave the door open for a third Callister episode. It might be for the best if Black Mirror gives the Callister concept a good rest before any temptation to do another is entertained because you'd probably need to come up with some good ideas and do something slightly different next time.

USS Callister: Into Infinity is a very entertaining end to what has generally been a good solid season Black Mirror. I wasn't a fan of Hotel Reverie but aside from that I found all the episodes in season seven interesting and highly watchable. The advantage of an anthology show is you can do whatever you want (within reason) from week to week. The show can bleak, it can be comedic, or it can be sentimental and optimistic. In theory this show could run forever. It's not a regular sort of show where in the end you run out of story or actors want to leave. Each new episode of Black Mirror has a different story and different cast. Black Mirror has created and sustained a fairly enviable position in the anthology television landscape because the competition is not exactly stellar. There is no Rod Serling's Twilight Zone, Night Gallery, Alfred Hitchcock Presents or Tales from the Crypt to go up against. The modern anthology shows (Guillermo del Toro's Cabinet of Curiosities, Creepshow, the 2019 Twilight Zone revival etc) just haven't clicked in the way that Black Mirror does at its best. The only equal Black Mirror has when it comes to modern anthology shows is the brilliant Inside No. 9 - which recently ended after nine seasons. There seems no reason why Black Mirror, drawing on ever changing technology headlines plucked from the real world, can't go on for many more years to come. And Black Mirror's cult status in popular culture is merely confirmed when good films like Ex Machina, M3GAN and Companion come along and are described by many as feeling like Black Mirror episodes. If that isn't praise I don't know what is.

Photo Credit

https://unsplash.com/photos/a-black-bug-on-a-blue-surface-NeK5dKVhnig

Katelyn G

September 13, 2022

Printed in Dunstable, United Kingdom